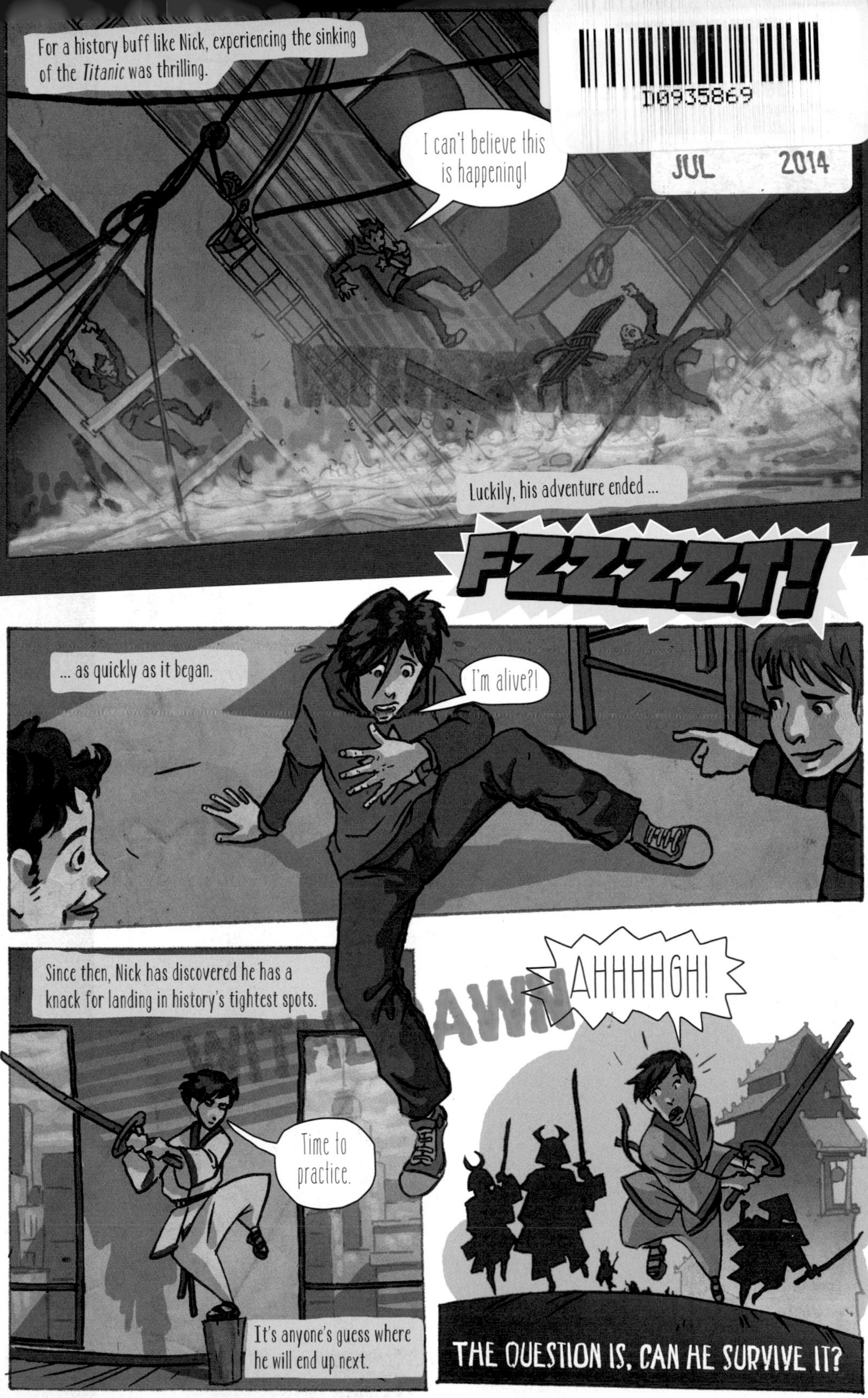
For a history buff like Nick, experiencing the sinking of the *Titanic* was thrilling.
I can't believe this is happening!
Luckily, his adventure ended ...
FZZZZT!
... as quickly as it began.
I'm alive?!
Since then, Nick has discovered he has a knack for landing in history's tightest spots.
Time to practice.
It's anyone's guess where he will end up next.
AHHHHGH!
THE QUESTION IS, CAN HE SURVIVE IT?

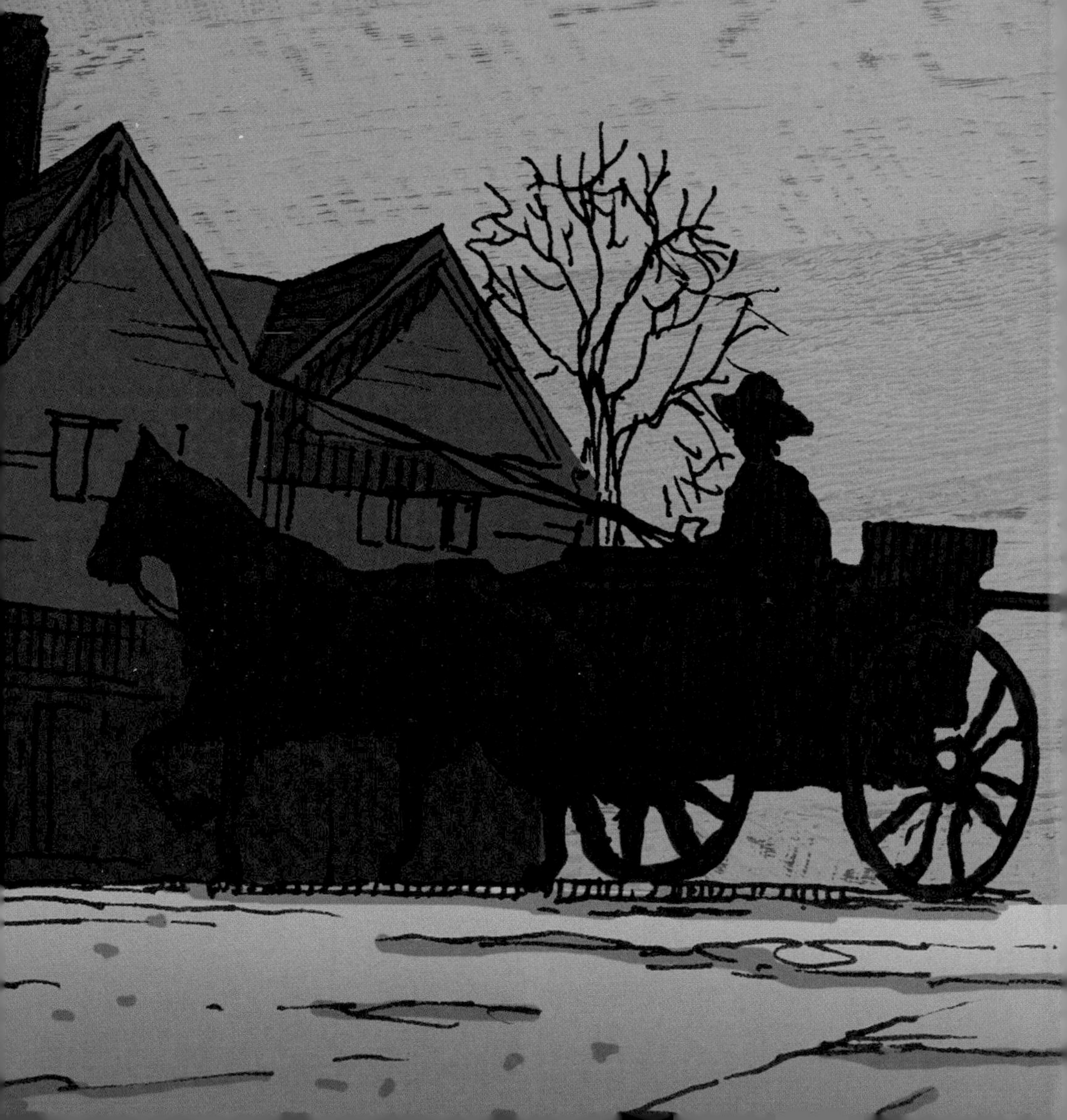

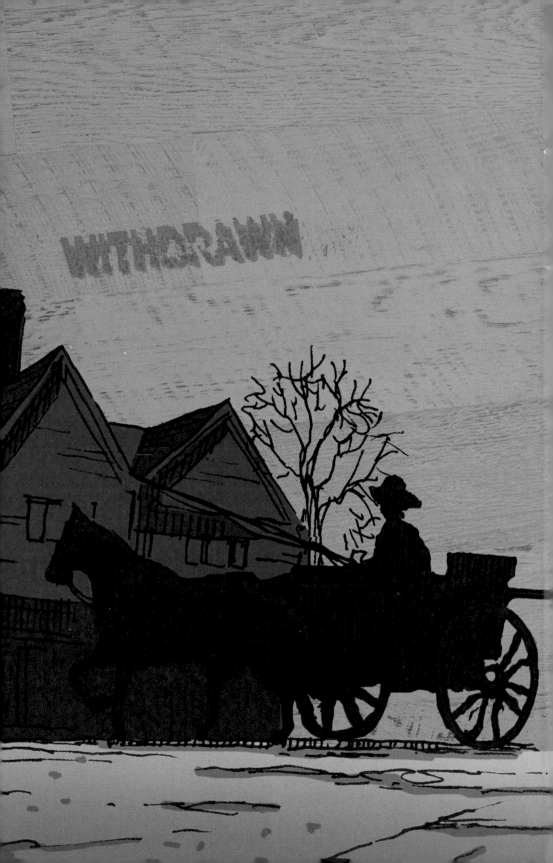

Nickolas Flux HISTORY CHRONICLES

ARRESTED FOR WITCHCRAFT!

NICKOLAS FLUX and the Salem Witch Trials

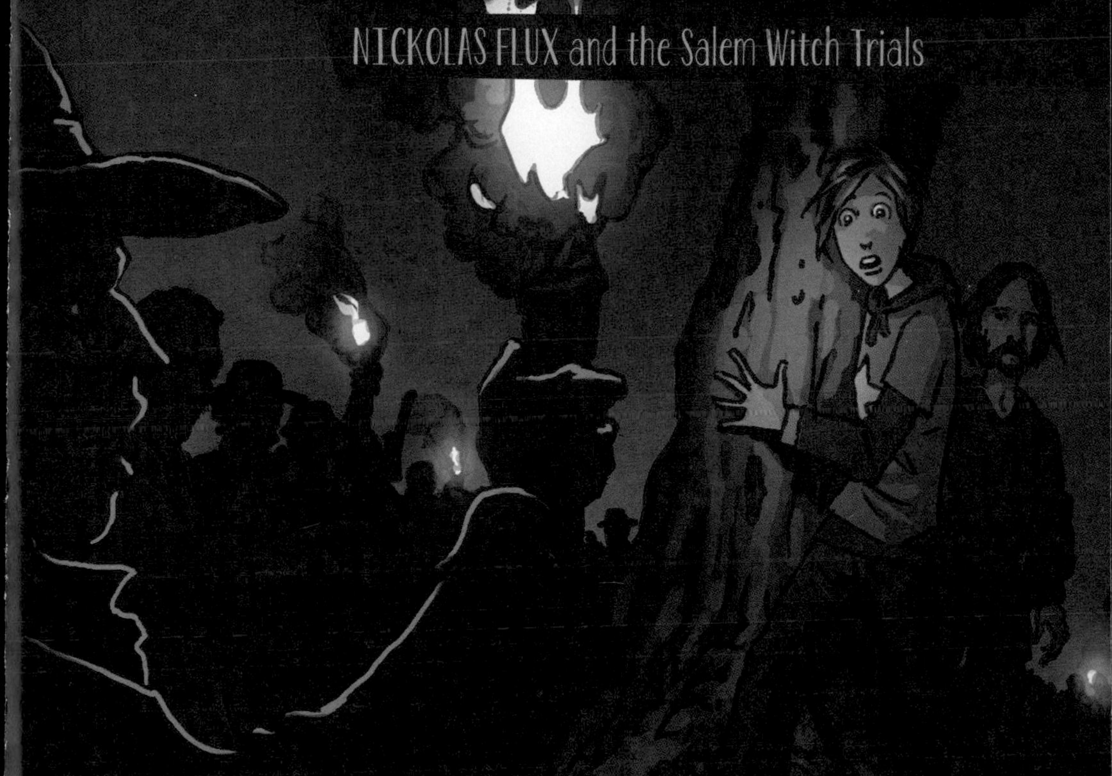

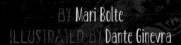

BY Mari Bolte

ILLUSTRATED BY Dante Ginevra

CONSULTANT:

Richard Bell, PhD

Associate Professor of History

University of Maryland, College Park

CAPSTONE PRESS

a capstone imprint

Graphic Library is published by Capstone Press,
1710 Roe Crest Drive, North Mankato, Minnesota 56003
www.capstonepub.com

Library of Congress Cataloging-in-Publication Data
Bolte, Mari.
Arrested for witchcraft! : Nickolas Flux and the Salem witch trials / Marissa Bolte ; illustrated by Dante Ginevra.
pages cm.—(Nickolas Flux history chronicles)
Summary: "When a spontaneous time leap sends Nickolas Flux back to Salem, Massachusetts, during the height of the witch trials, what's a teenage history buff to do? Try to avoid being tried for witchcraft, of course! From meeting accused witches to running from angry mobs, Nick must survive one of the most frightening moments in American history"—Provided by publisher.
Includes bibliographical references.
ISBN 978-1-4765-3947-8 (library binding)
ISBN 978-1-4765-5151-7 (paperback)
ISBN 978-1-4765-6008-3 (eBook PDF)
1. Trials (Witchcraft)—Massachusetts—Salem—Juvenile fiction. 2. Graphic novels. [1. Graphic novels. 2. Trials (Witchcraft)—Fiction. 3. Witchcraft—Fiction. 4. Salem (Mass.)—History—Colonial period, ca. 1600-1775—Fiction. 5. Time travel—Fiction.] I. Ginevra, Dante, 1976- illustrator. II. Title.
PZ7.7.B64Ar 2014
741.5'973—dc23 2013038645

Photo Credits:
Design Elements: Shutterstock (backgrounds)

Editor's note:
Direct quotations, noted in red type, appear on the following pages:
Pages 20, 24, and 25 from *A Delusion of Satan: The Full Story of the Salem Witch Trials* by Frances Hill (New York: Doubleday, 1995).

EDITOR
Adrian Vigliano

DESIGNER
Ashlee Suker

ART DIRECTOR
Nathan Gassman

PRODUCTION SPECIALIST
Kathy McColley

Printed in the United States of America in Stevens Point, Wisconsin.
092013 007767WZS14

TABLE OF CONTENTS

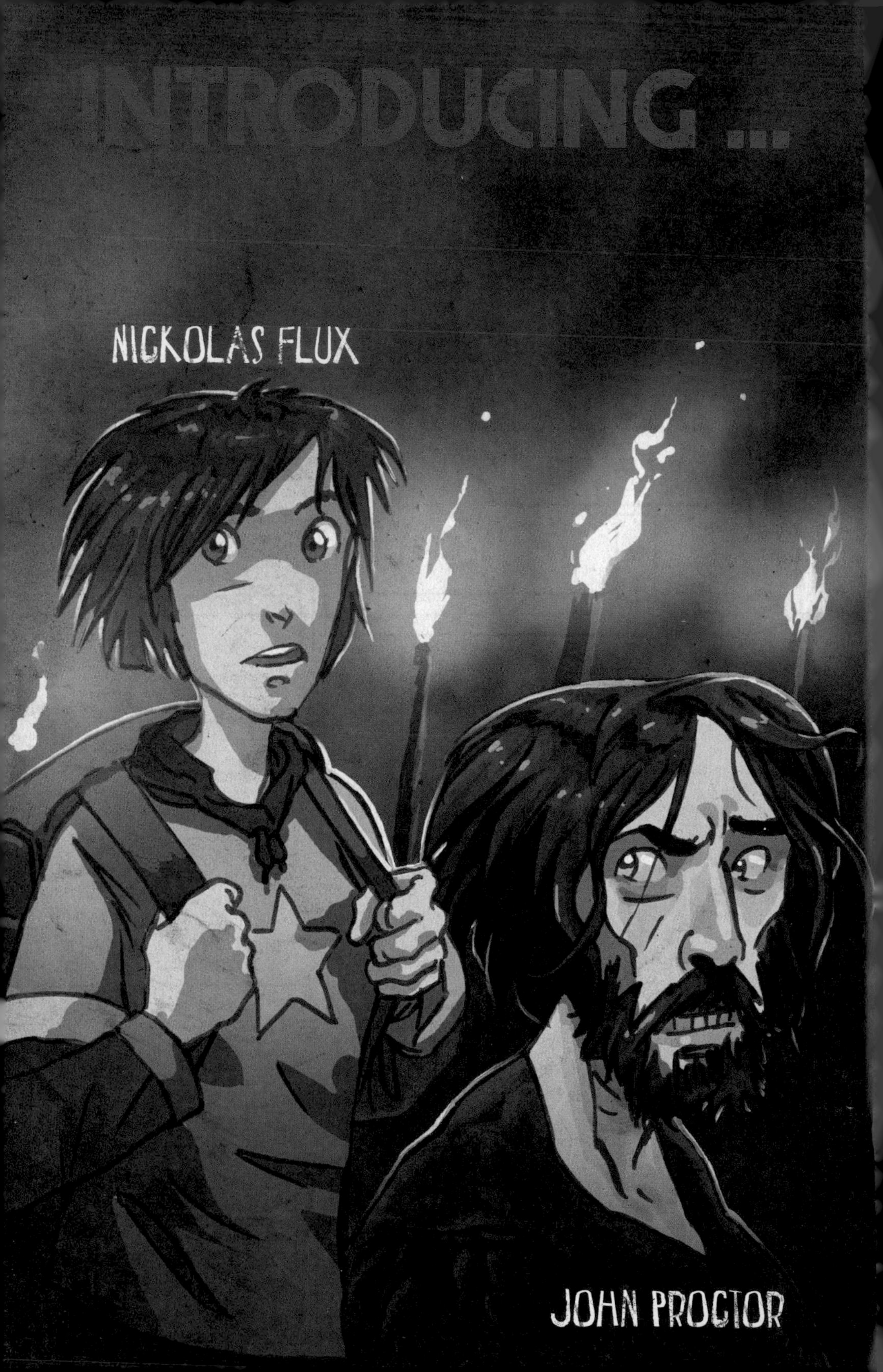
INTRODUCING ...
NICKOLAS FLUX
JOHN PROCTOR

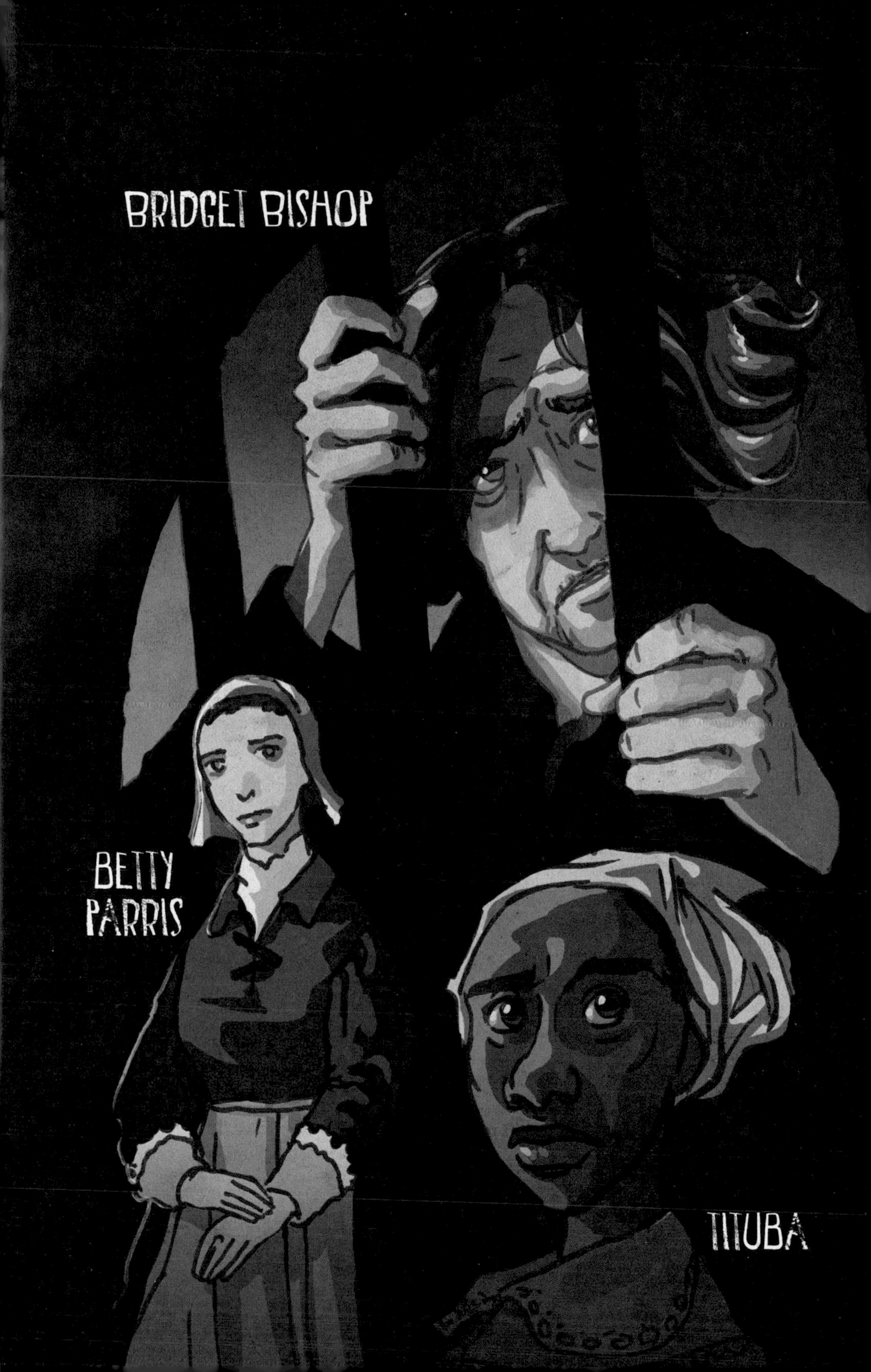
BRIDGET BISHOP
BETTY
PARRIS
TITUBA

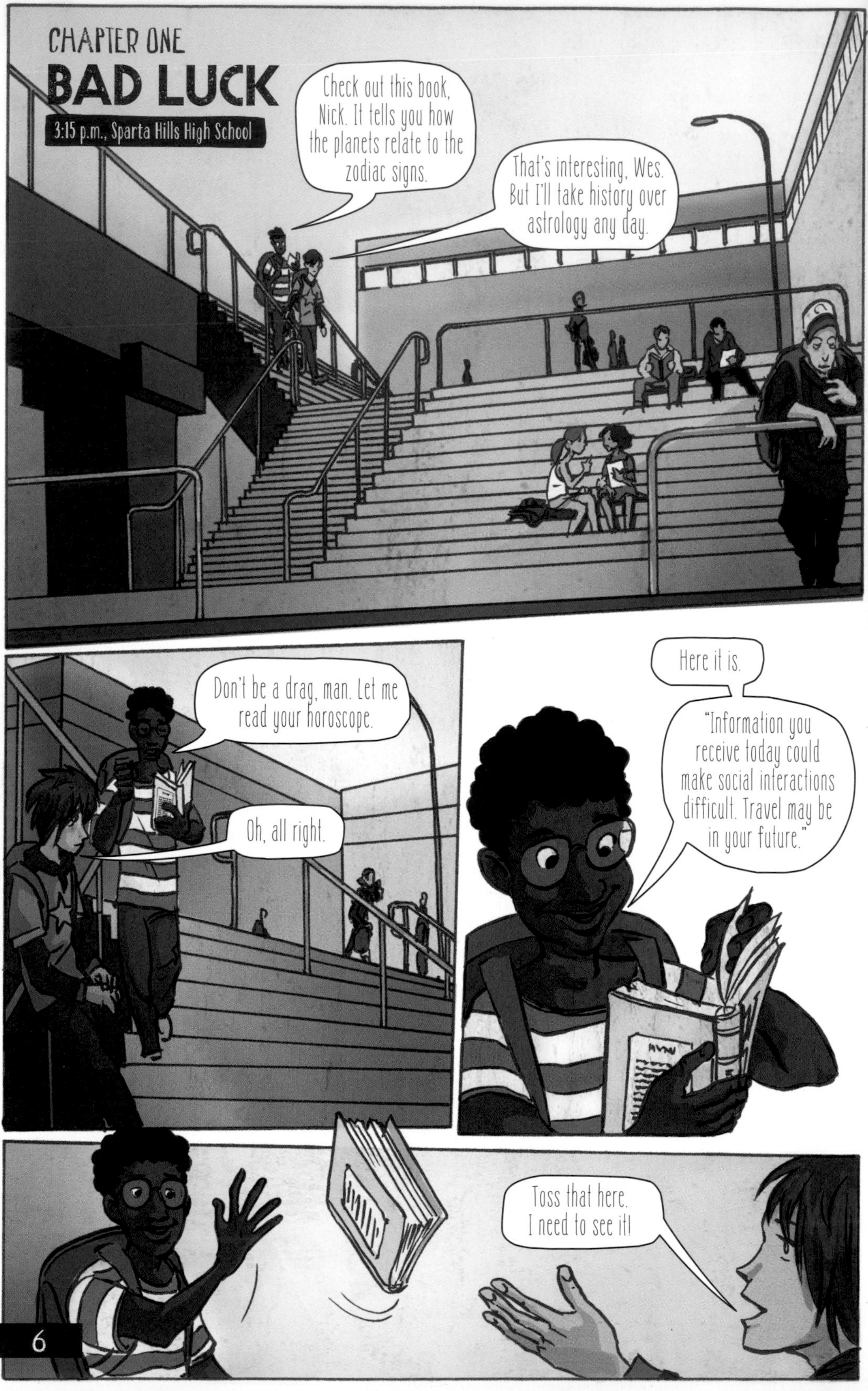
CHAPTER ONE
BAD LUCK
3:15 p.m., Sparta Hills High School
Check out this book, Nick. It tells you how the planets relate to the zodiac signs.
That's interesting, Wes. But I'll take history over astrology any day.
Don't be a drag, man. Let me read your horoscope.
Oh, all right.
Here it is.
"Information you receive today could make social interactions difficult. Travel may be in your future."
Toss that here. I need to see it!

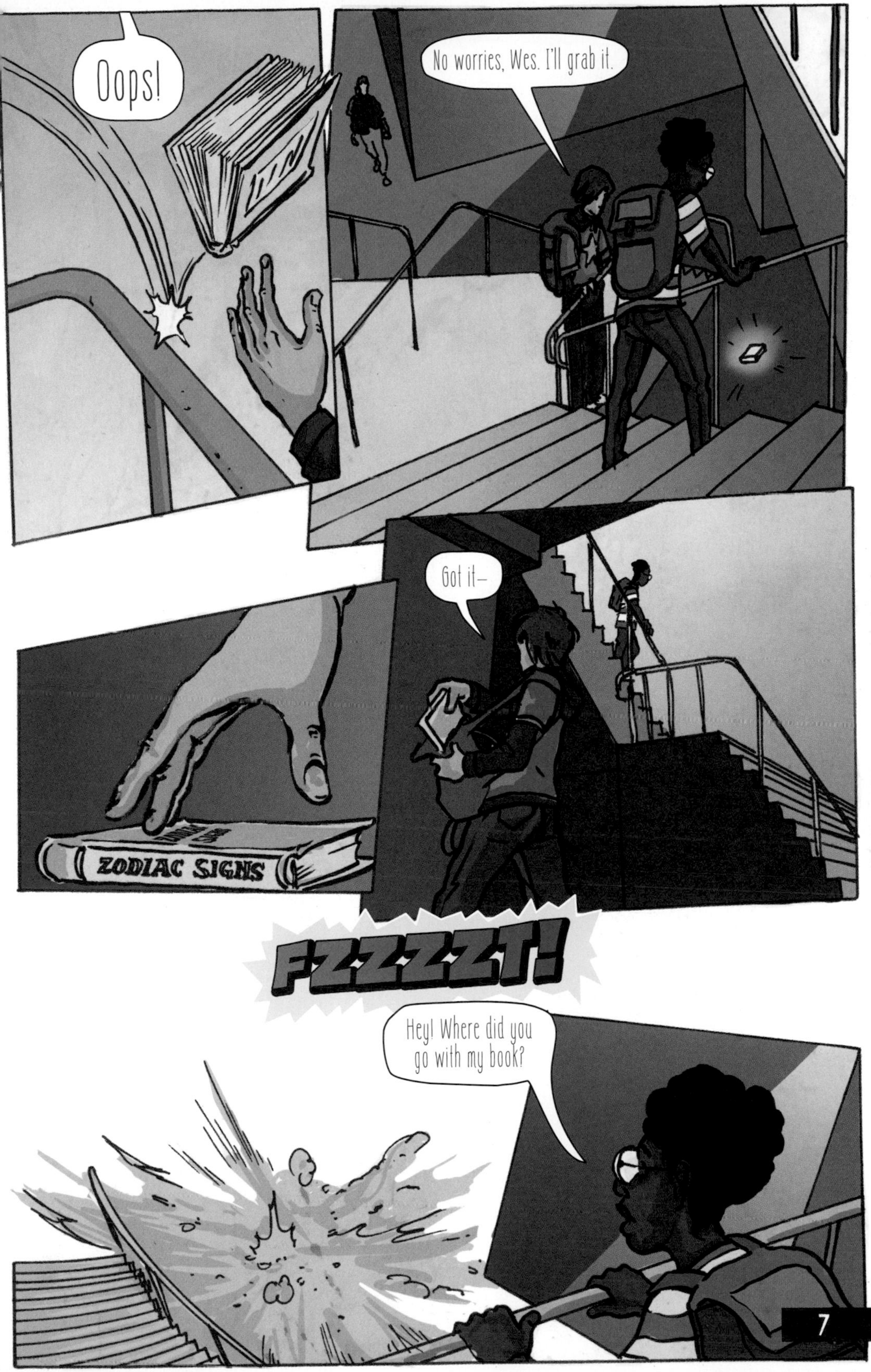
Oops!
No worries, Wes. I'll grab it.
ZODIAC SIGNS
Got it—
FZZZZT!
Hey! Where did you go with my book?

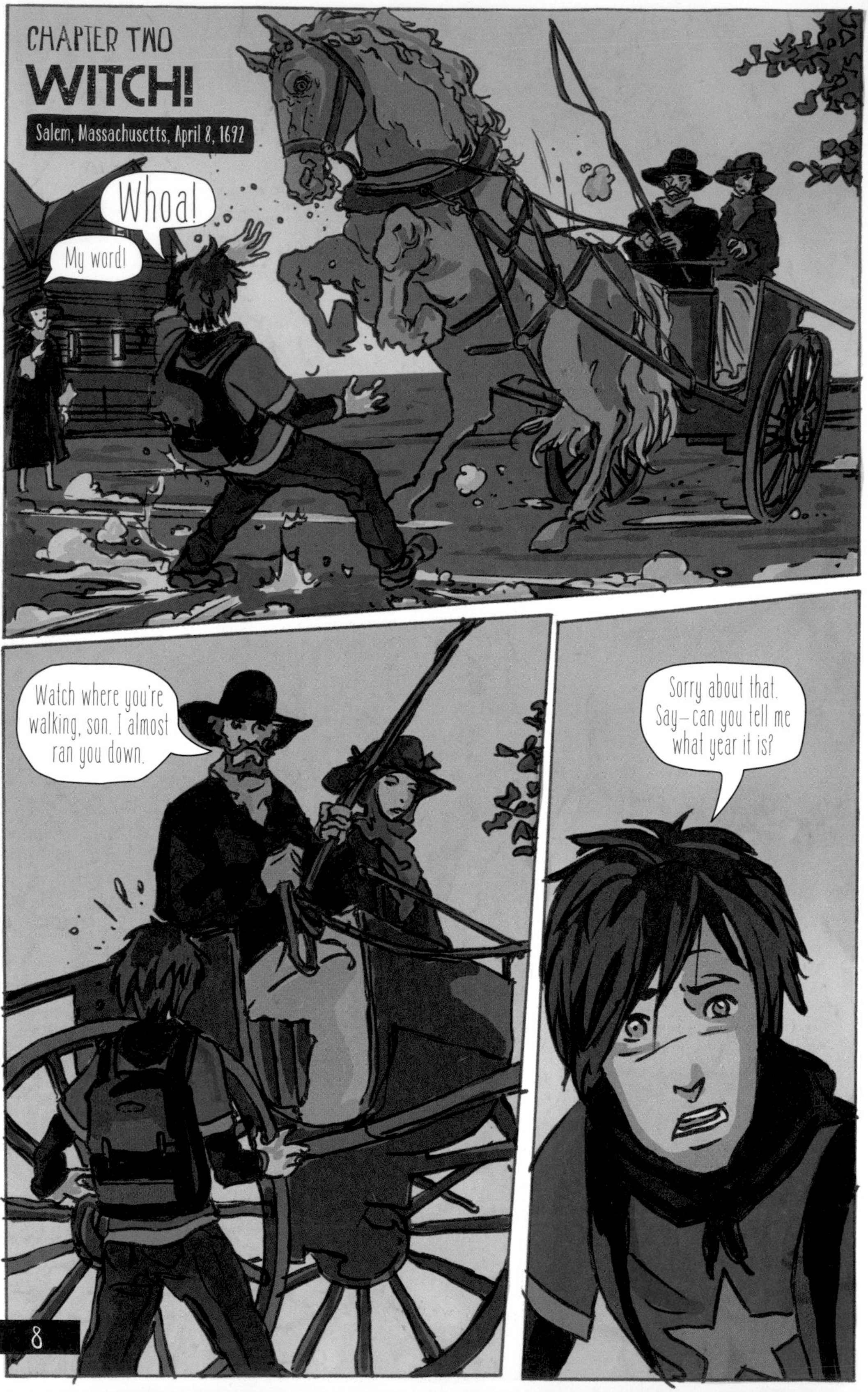
CHAPTER TWO
WITCH!
Salem, Massachusetts, April 8, 1692
Whoa!
My word!
Watch where you're walking, son. I almost ran you down.
Sorry about that. Say—can you tell me what year it is?

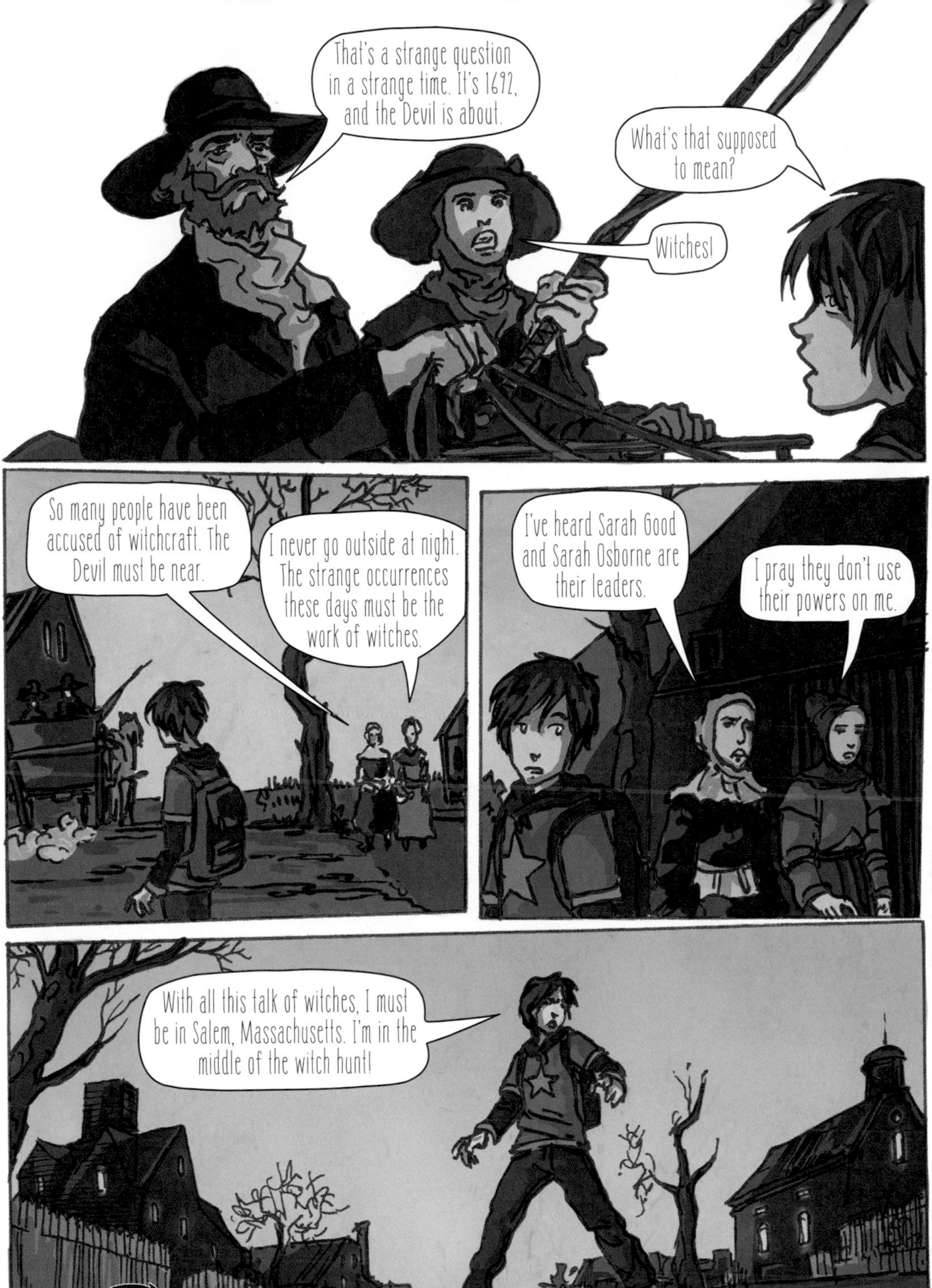
That's a strange question in a strange time. It's 1692, and the Devil is about.
What's that supposed to mean?
Witches!
So many people have been accused of witchcraft. The Devil must be near.
I never go outside at night. The strange occurrences these days must be the work of witches.
I've heard Sarah Good and Sarah Osborne are their leaders.
I pray they don't use their powers on me.
With all this talk of witches, I must be in Salem, Massachusetts. I'm in the middle of the witch hunt!

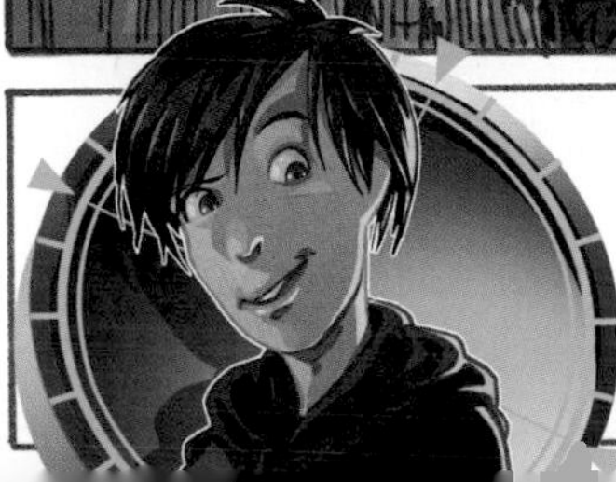

FLUX FACT

The Salem Witch Trials occurred between January 1692 and May 1693.

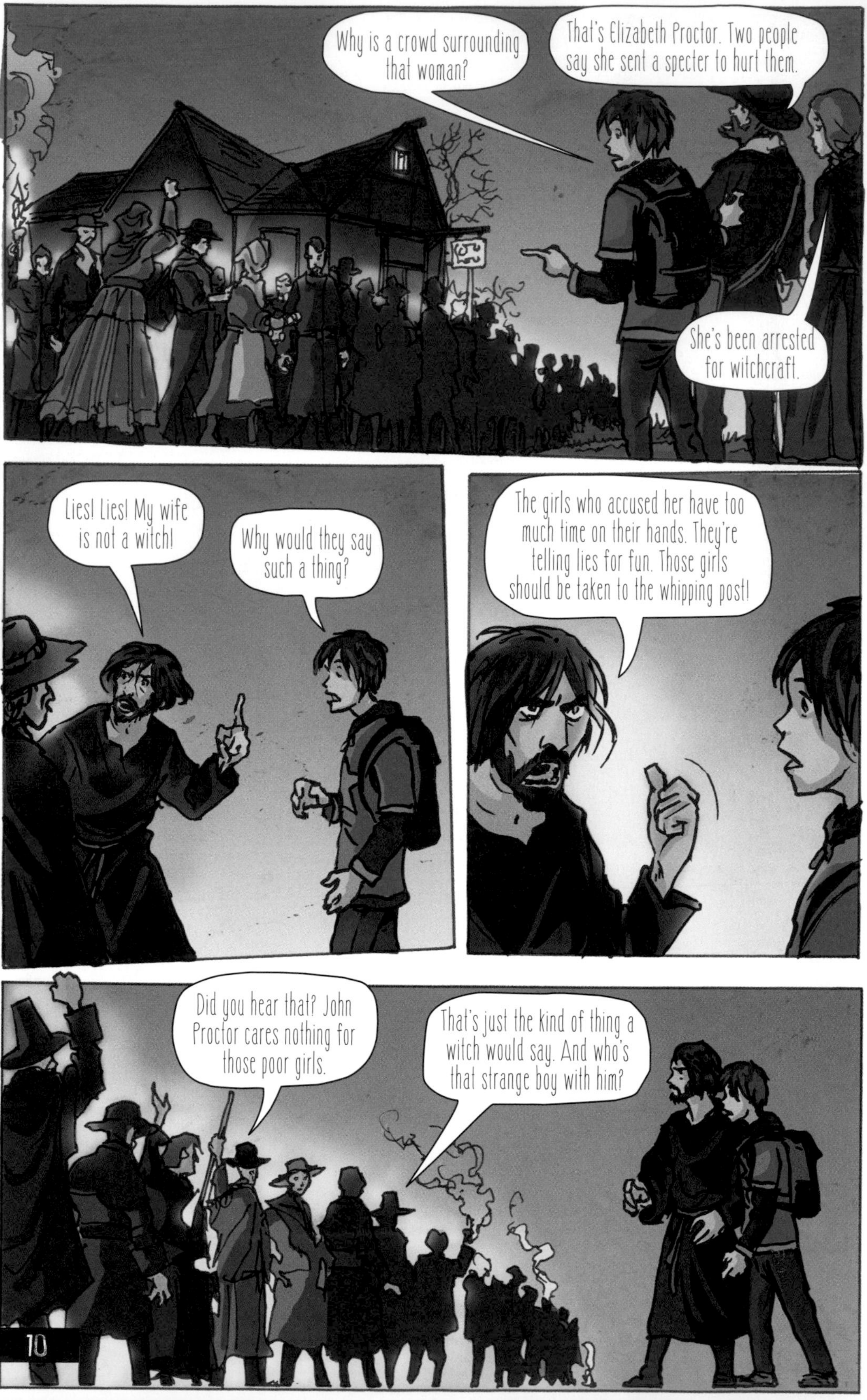

Why is a crowd surrounding that woman?
That's Elizabeth Proctor. Two people say she sent a specter to hurt them.
She's been arrested for witchcraft.
Lies! Lies! My wife is not a witch!
Why would they say such a thing?
The girls who accused her have too much time on their hands. They're telling lies for fun. Those girls should be taken to the whipping post!
Did you hear that? John Proctor cares nothing for those poor girls.
That's just the kind of thing a witch would say. And who's that strange boy with him?

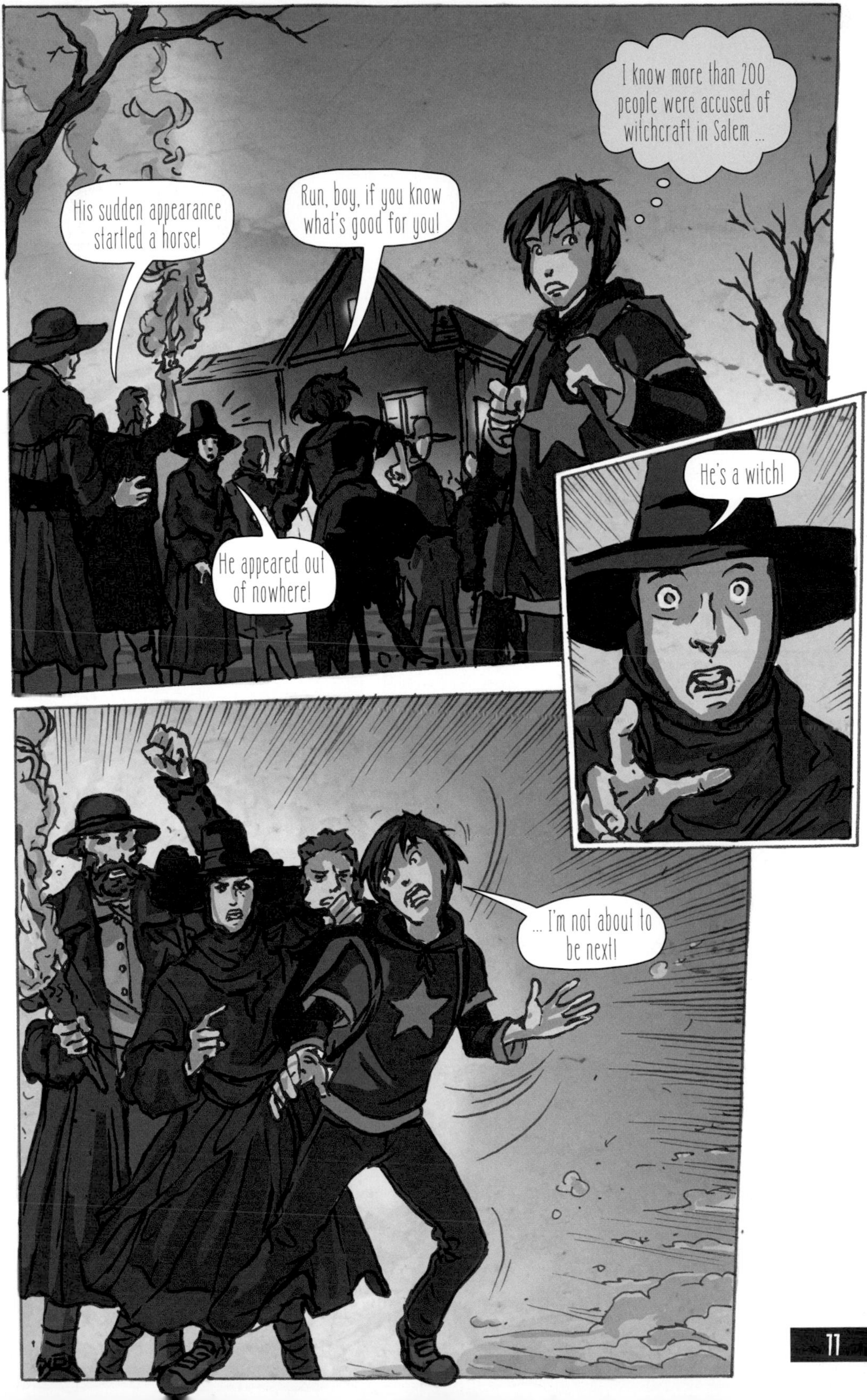
I know more than 200 people were accused of witchcraft in Salem ...
His sudden appearance startled a horse!
Run, boy, if you know what's good for you!
He appeared out of nowhere!
He's a witch!
... I'm not about to be next!

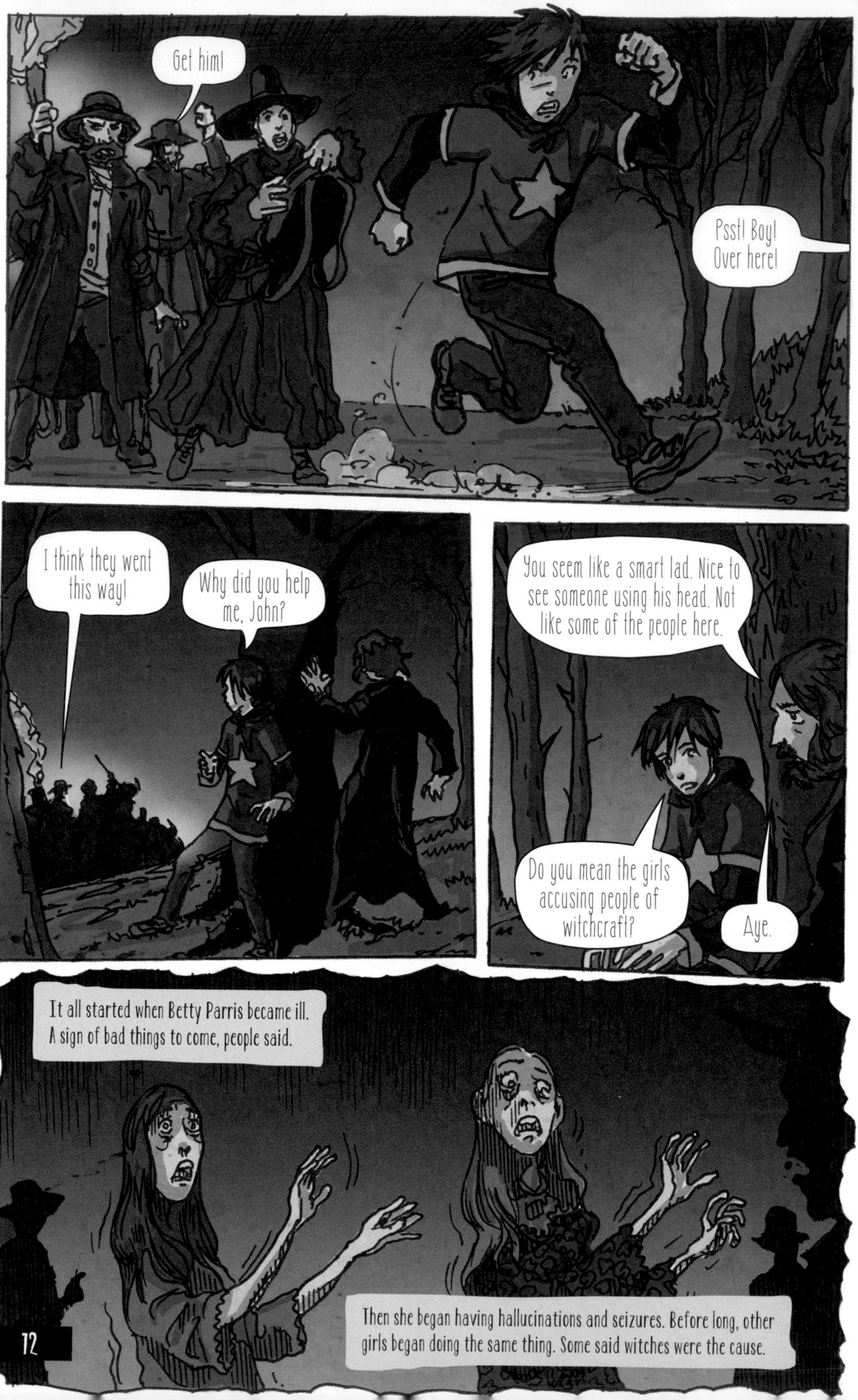
Get him!
Psst! Boy! Over here!
I think they went this way!
Why did you help me, John?
You seem like a smart lad. Nice to see someone using his head. Not like some of the people here.
Do you mean the girls accusing people of witchcraft?
Aye.
It all started when Betty Parris became ill. A sign of bad things to come, people said.
Then she began having hallucinations and seizures. Before long, other girls began doing the same thing. Some said witches were the cause.

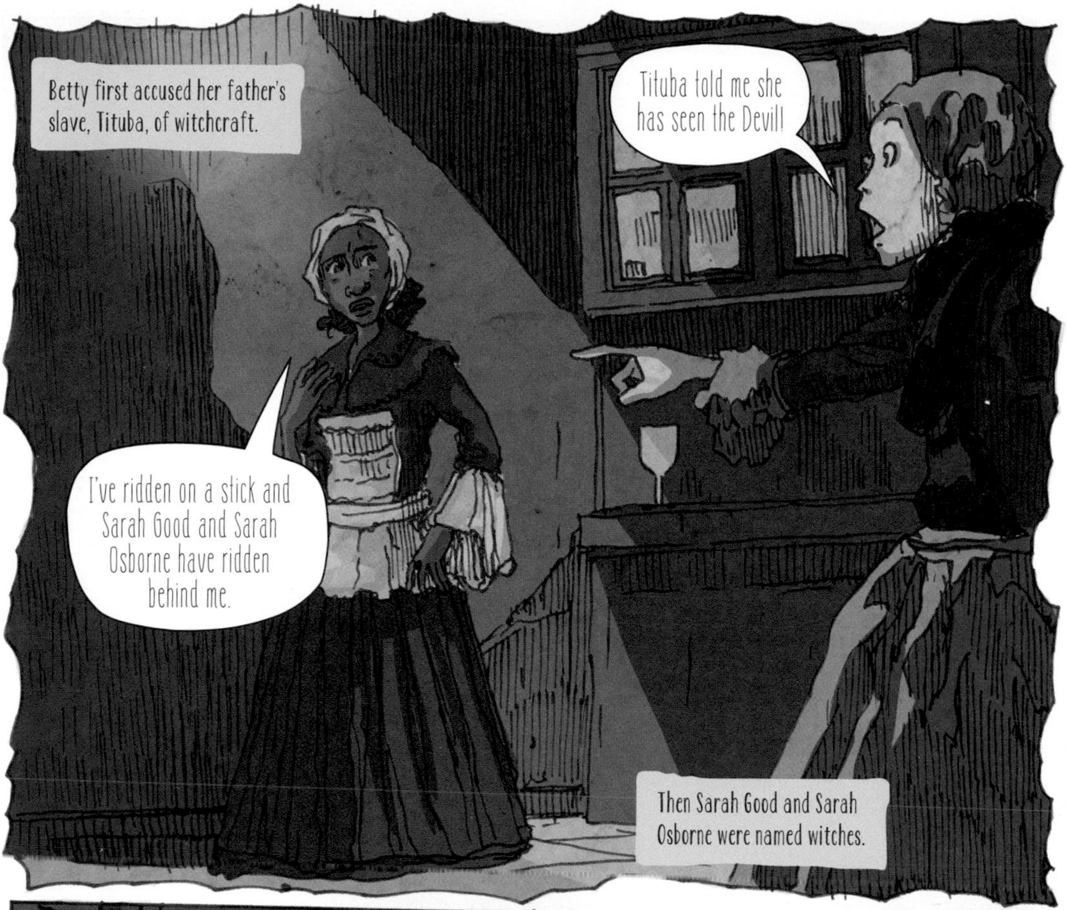
Betty first accused her father's slave, Tituba, of witchcraft.
Tituba told me she has seen the Devil!
I've ridden on a stick and Sarah Good and Sarah Osborne have ridden behind me.
Then Sarah Good and Sarah Osborne were named witches.

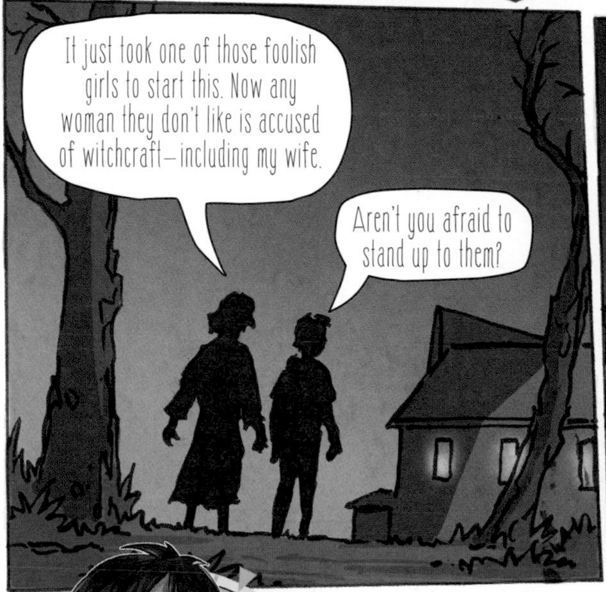
It just took one of those foolish girls to start this. Now any woman they don't like is accused of witchcraft—including my wife.
Aren't you afraid to stand up to them?

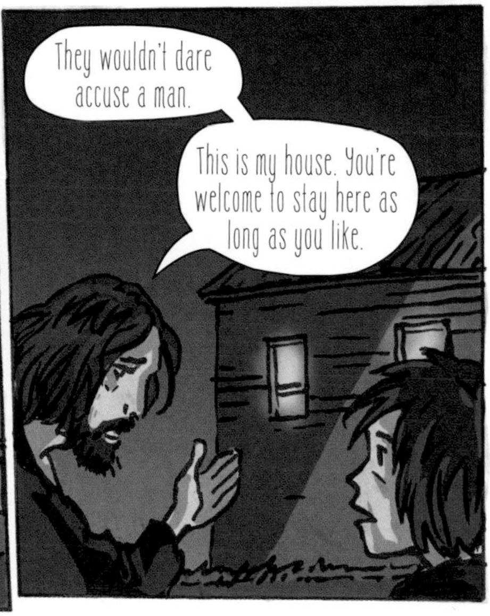
They wouldn't dare accuse a man.
This is my house. You're welcome to stay here as long as you like.

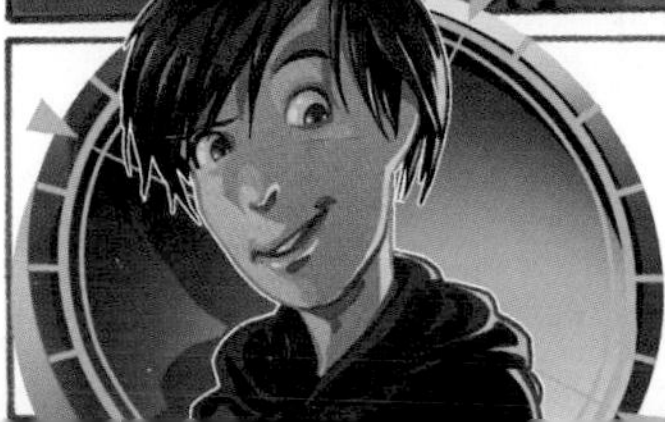

FLUX FACT

Tituba was the first suspected witch to confess. She was jailed but not tried or executed.

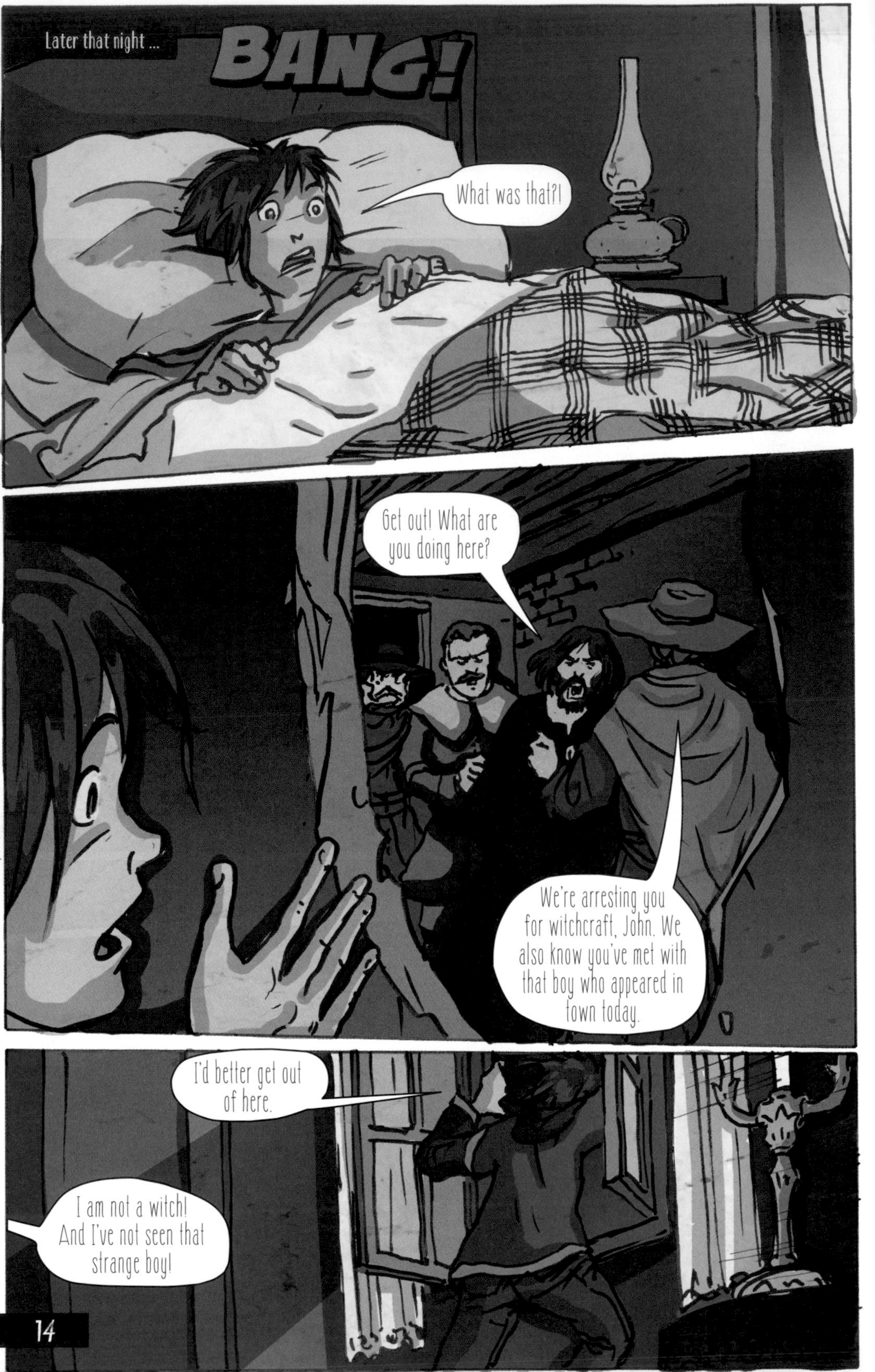
Later that night ...
BANG!
What was that?!
Get out! What are you doing here?
We're arresting you for witchcraft, John. We also know you've met with that boy who appeared in town today.
I'd better get out of here.
I am not a witch! And I've not seen that strange boy!

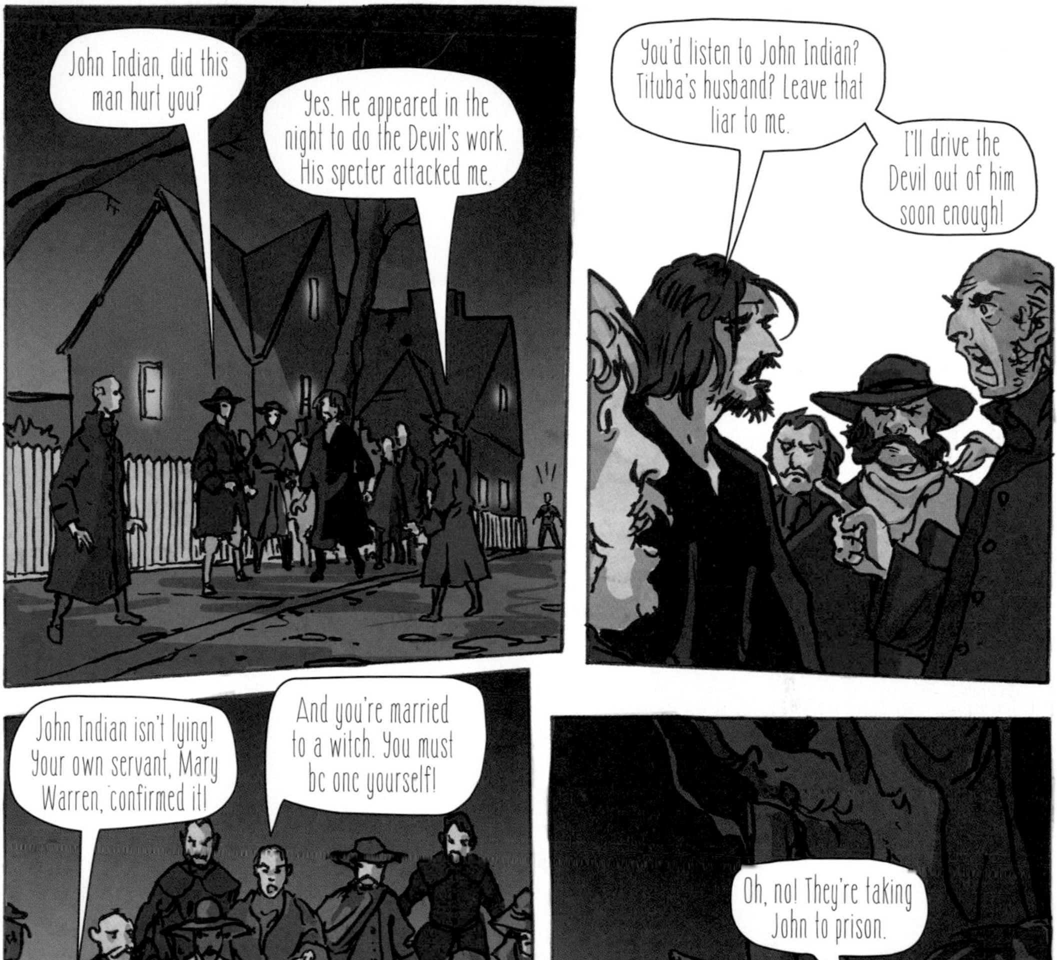
John Indian, did this man hurt you?
Yes. He appeared in the night to do the Devil's work. His specter attacked me.
You'd listen to John Indian? Tituba's husband? Leave that liar to me.
I'll drive the Devil out of him soon enough!
John Indian isn't lying! Your own servant, Mary Warren, confirmed it!
And you're married to a witch. You must bc onc yourself!
Oh, no! They're taking John to prison.

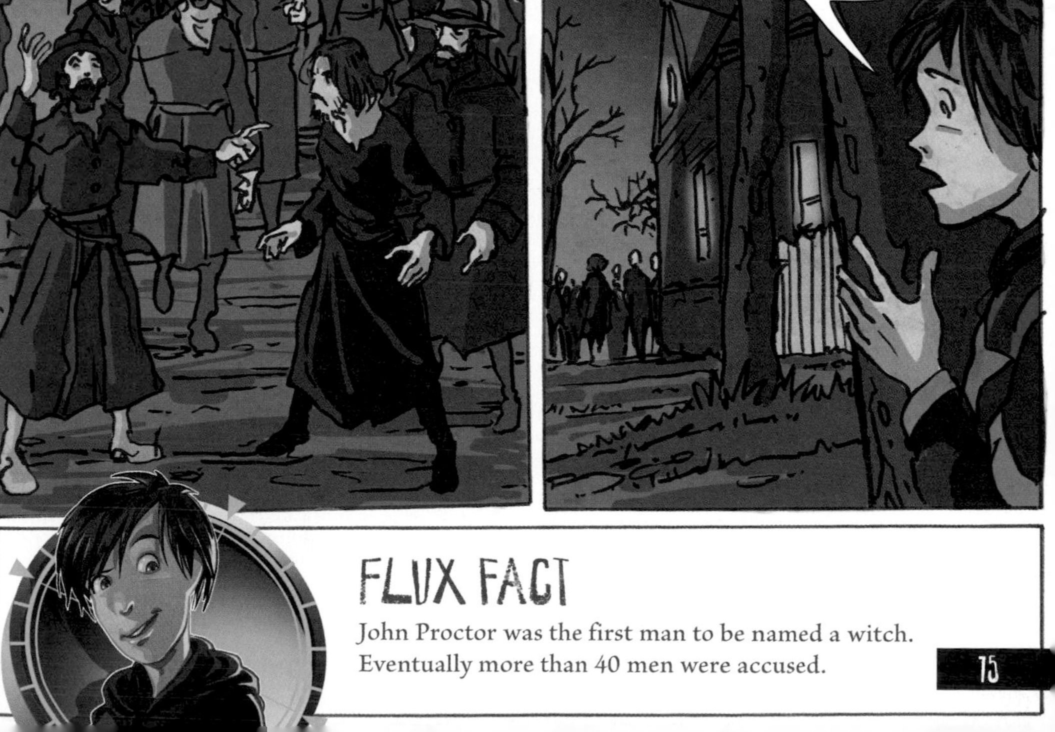

FLUX FACT

John Proctor was the first man to be named a witch. Eventually more than 40 men were accused.

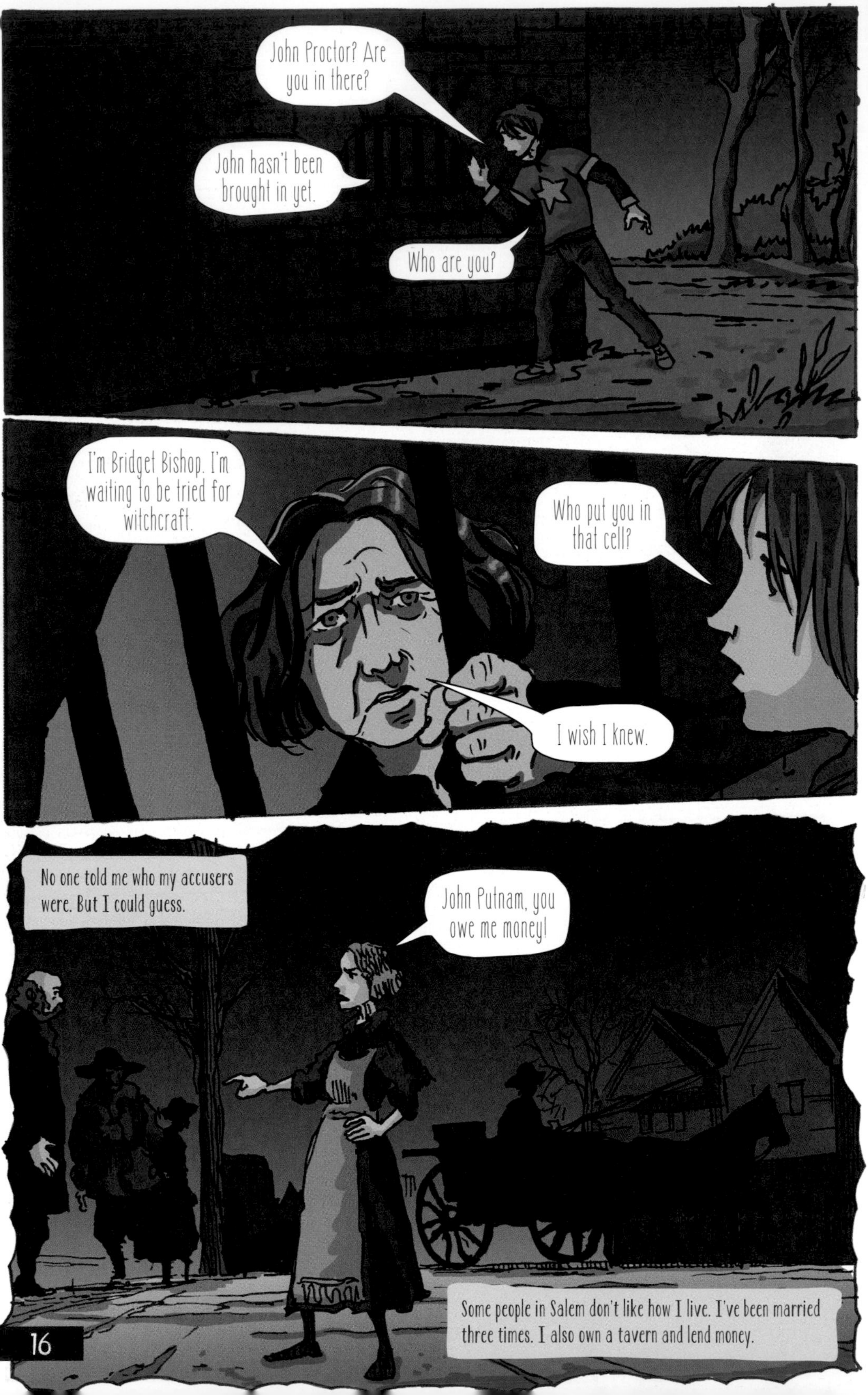

John Proctor? Are you in there?
John hasn't been brought in yet.
Who are you?
I'm Bridget Bishop. I'm waiting to be tried for witchcraft.
Who put you in that cell?
I wish I knew.
No one told me who my accusers were. But I could guess.
John Putnam, you owe me money!
Some people in Salem don't like how I live. I've been married three times. I also own a tavern and lend money.

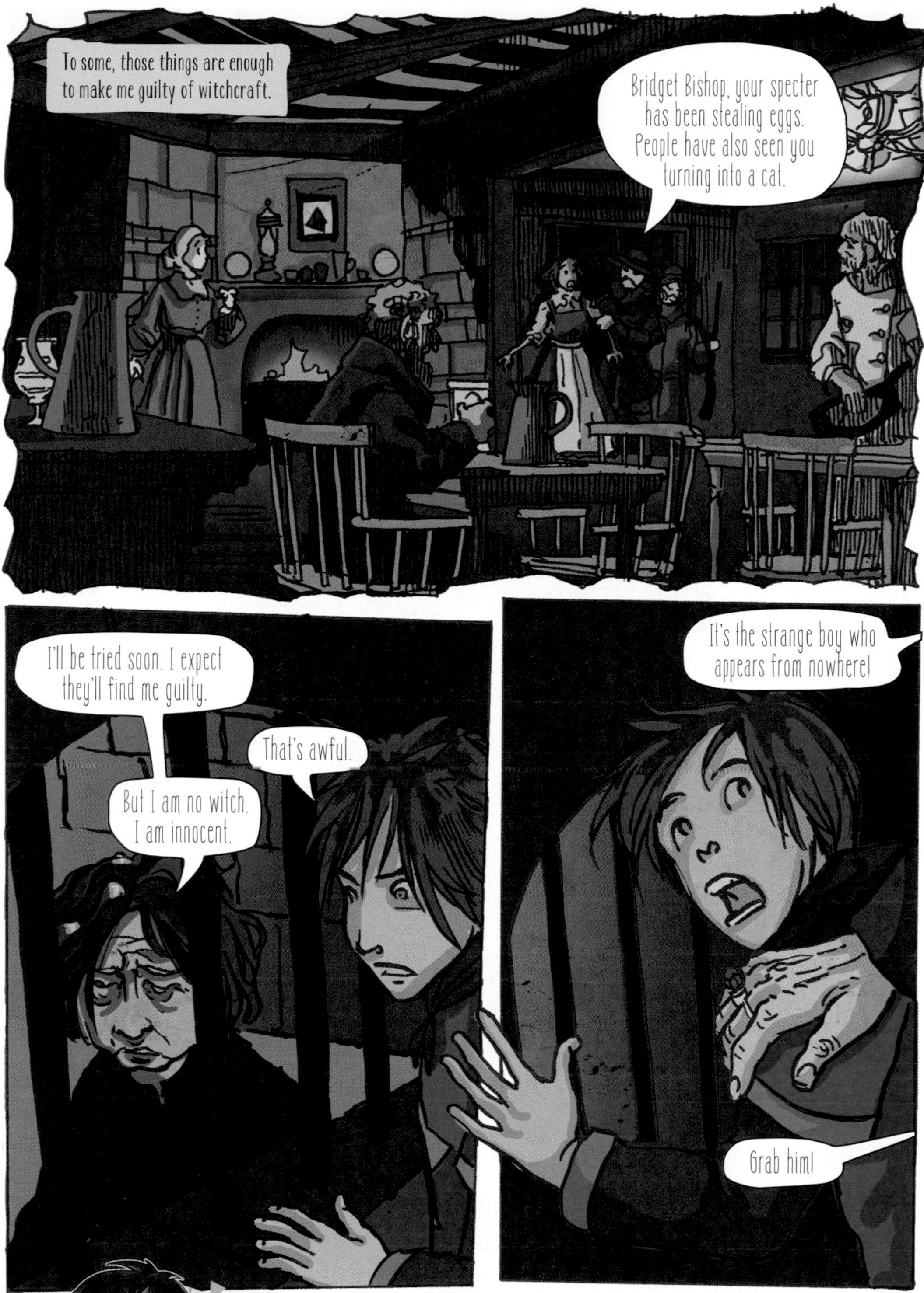
To some, those things are enough to make me guilty of witchcraft.
Bridget Bishop, your specter has been stealing eggs. People have also seen you turning into a cat.
I'll be tried soon. I expect they'll find me guilty.
But I am no witch. I am innocent.
That's awful.
It's the strange boy who appears from nowhere!
Grab him!

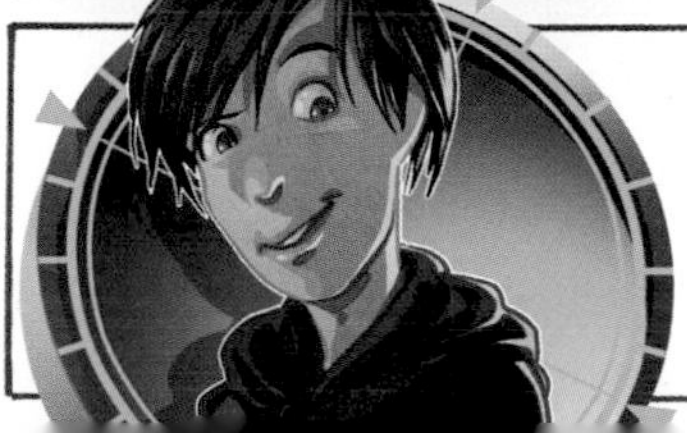

FLUX FACT

The Putnams were a powerful family in Salem. Their evidence led to the trials of Tituba, Sarah Good, and Sarah Osborne.

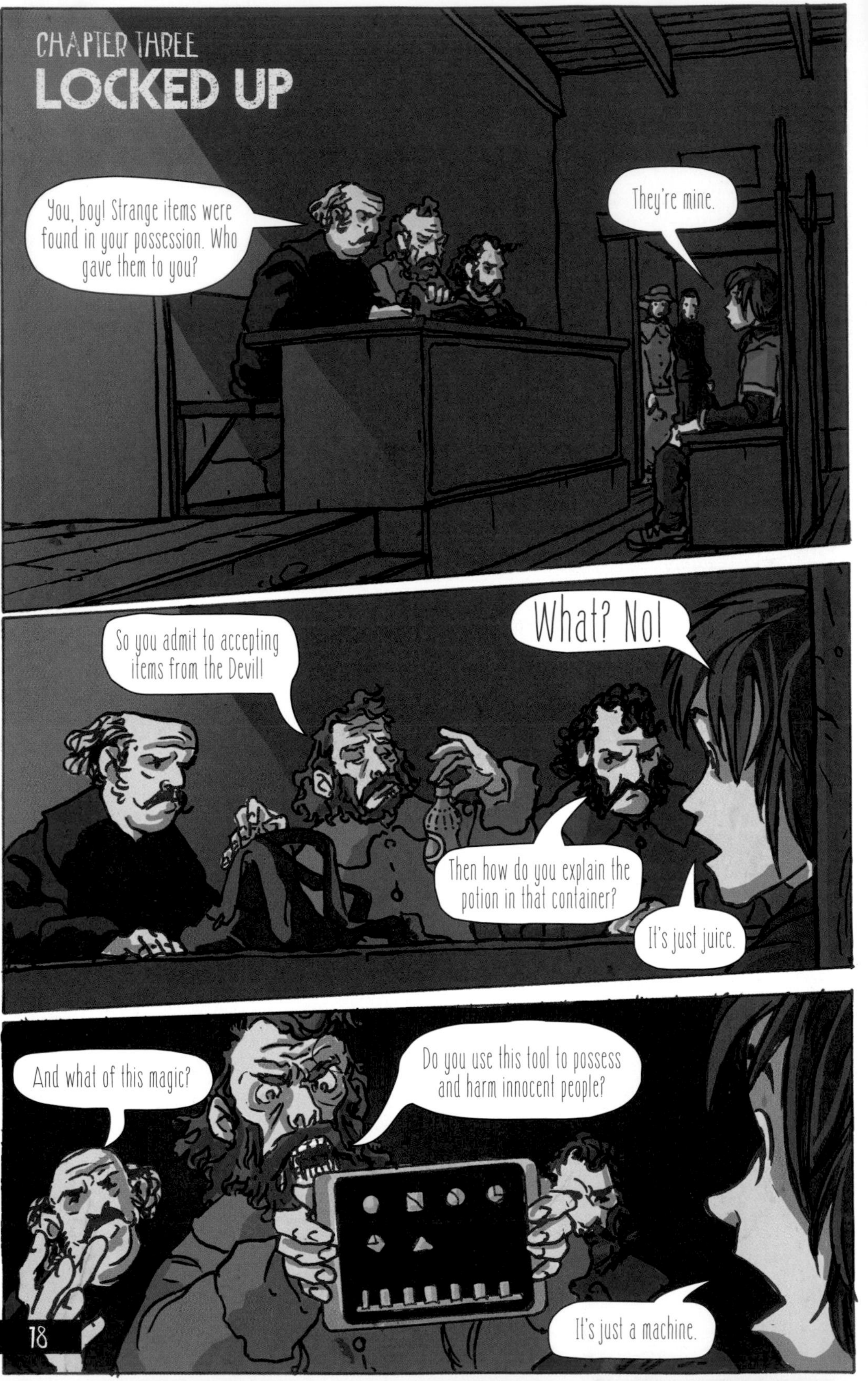
CHAPTER THREE
LOCKED UP
You, boy! Strange items were found in your possession. Who gave them to you?
They're mine.
So you admit to accepting items from the Devil!
What? No!
Then how do you explain the potion in that container?
It's just juice.
And what of this magic?
Do you use this tool to possess and harm innocent people?
It's just a machine.

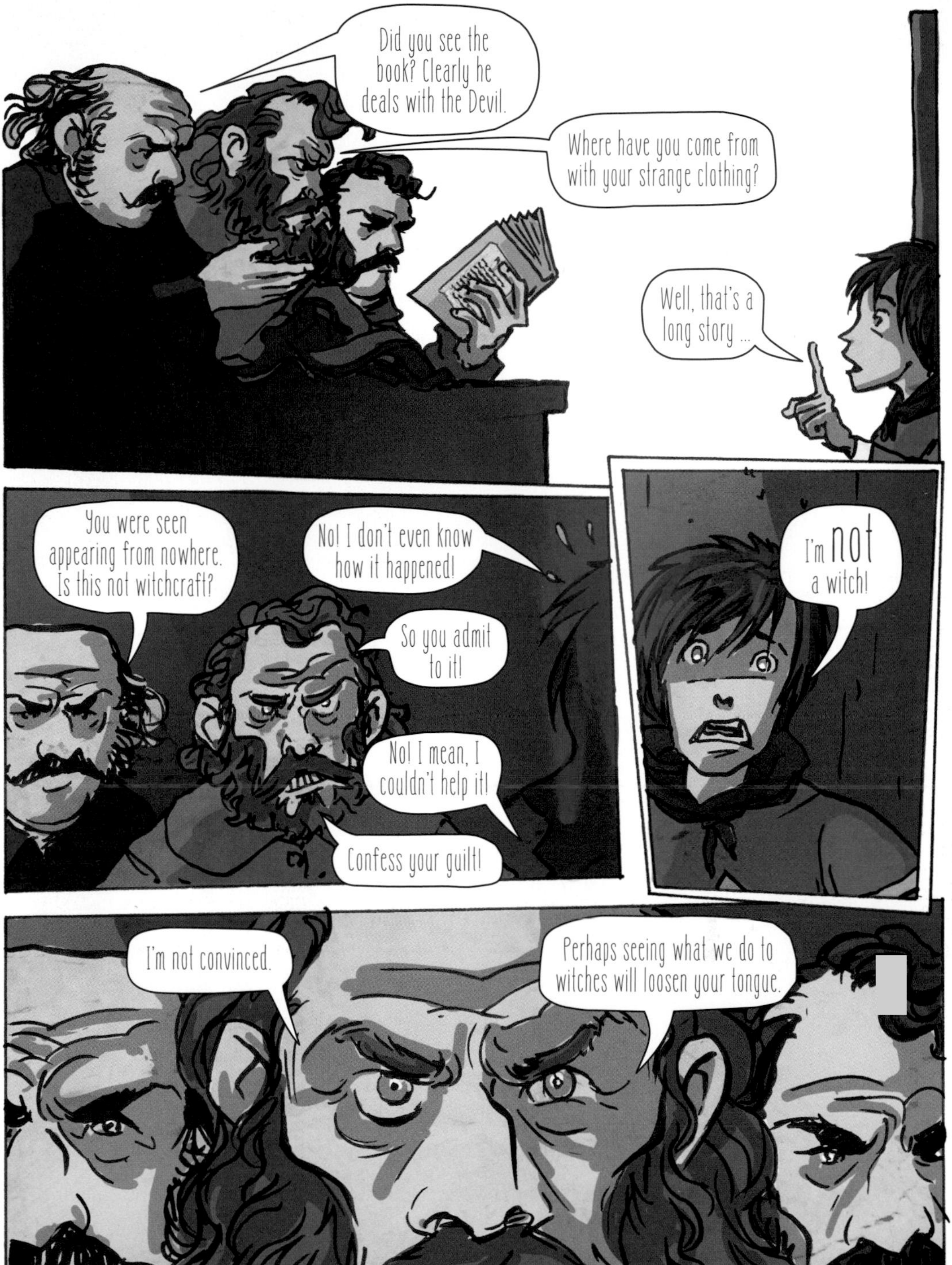
Did you see the book? Clearly he deals with the Devil.
Where have you come from with your strange clothing?
Well, that's a long story ...
You were seen appearing from nowhere. Is this not witchcraft?
No! I don't even know how it happened!
So you admit to it!
No! I mean, I couldn't help it!
Confess your guilt!
I'm not a witch!
I'm not convinced.
Perhaps seeing what we do to witches will loosen your tongue.

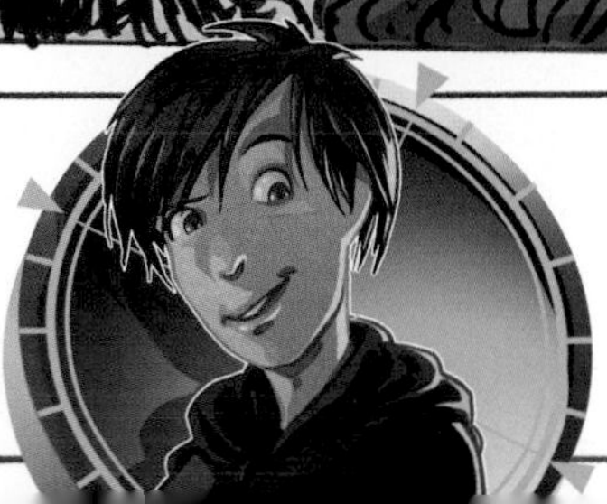

FLUX FACT

Accused witches could be tortured for a confession. One accused witch, Giles Corey, refused a trial. The penalty was being pressed to death. Heavy stones were piled on top of him until he died.

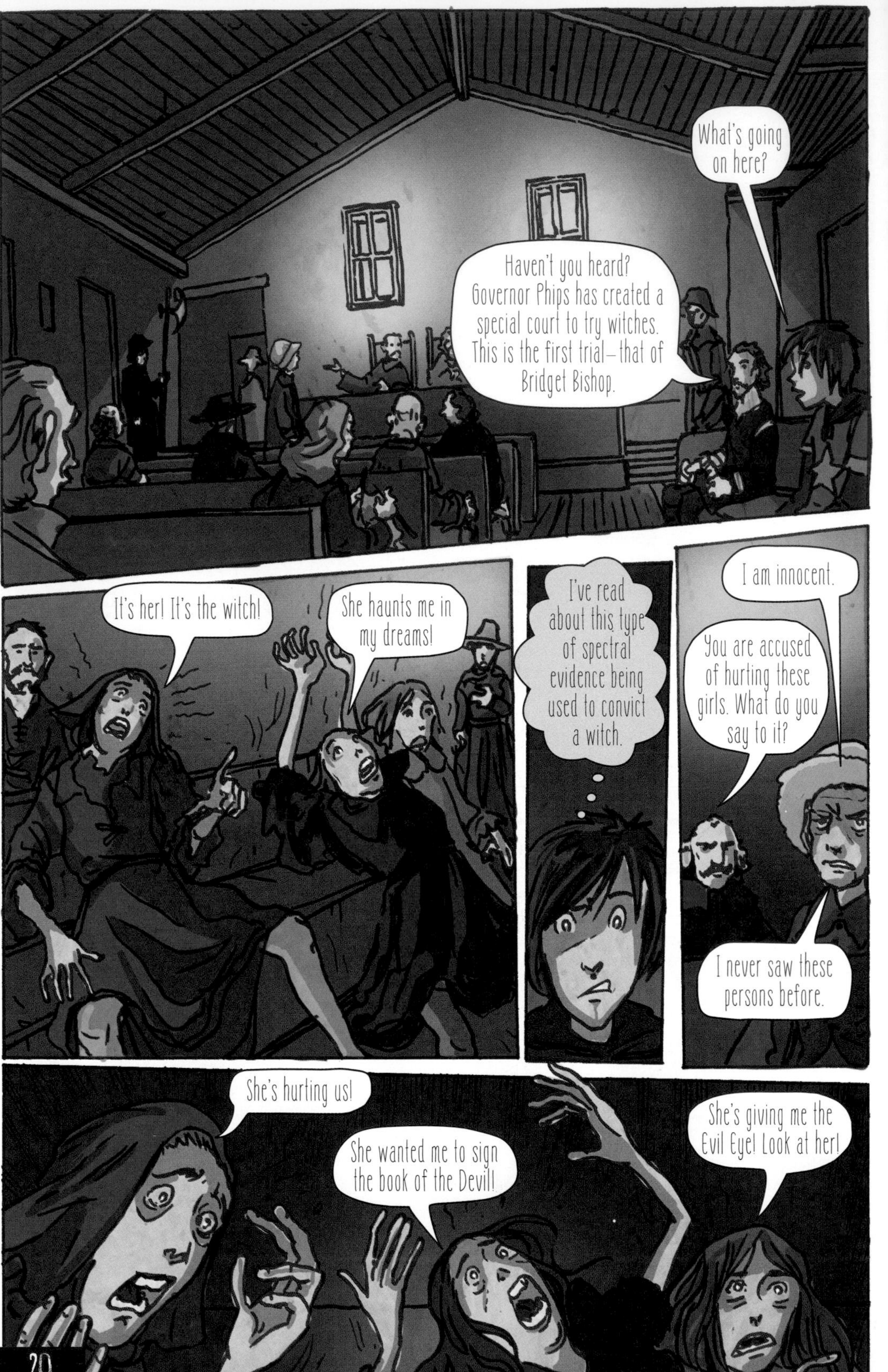

What's going on here?
Haven't you heard? Governor Phips has created a special court to try witches. This is the first trial—that of Bridget Bishop.
It's her! It's the witch!
She haunts me in my dreams!
I've read about this type of spectral evidence being used to convict a witch.
I am innocent.
You are accused of hurting these girls. What do you say to it?
I never saw these persons before.
She's hurting us!
She wanted me to sign the book of the Devil!
She's giving me the Evil Eye! Look at her!

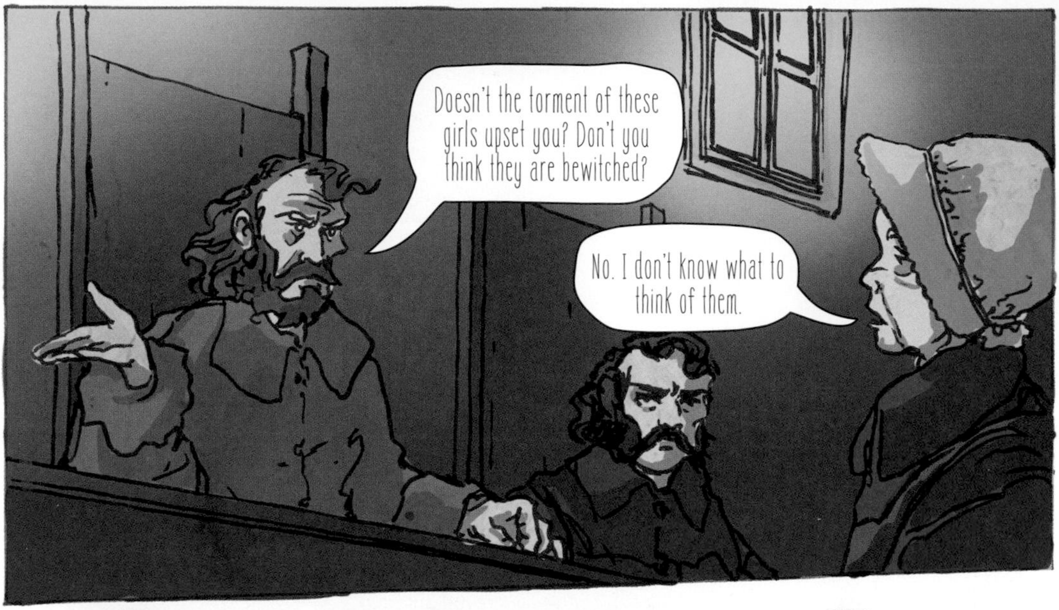

Doesn't the torment of these girls upset you? Don't you think they are bewitched?
No. I don't know what to think of them.

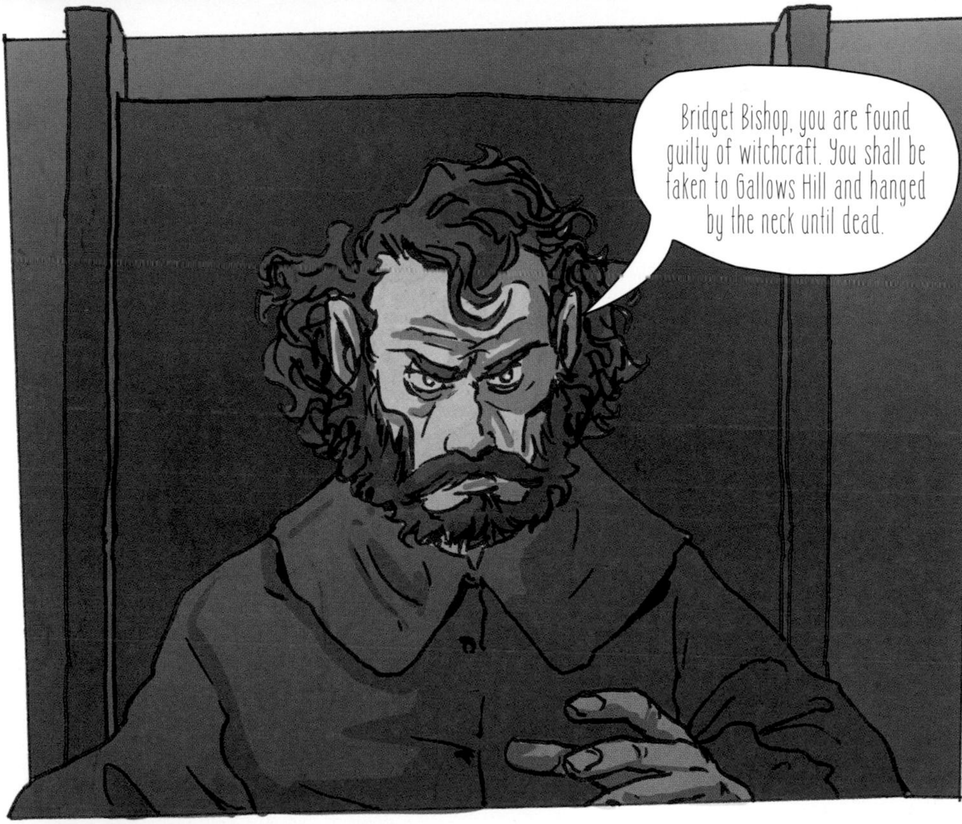

Bridget Bishop, you are found guilty of witchcraft. You shall be taken to Gallows Hill and hanged by the neck until dead.

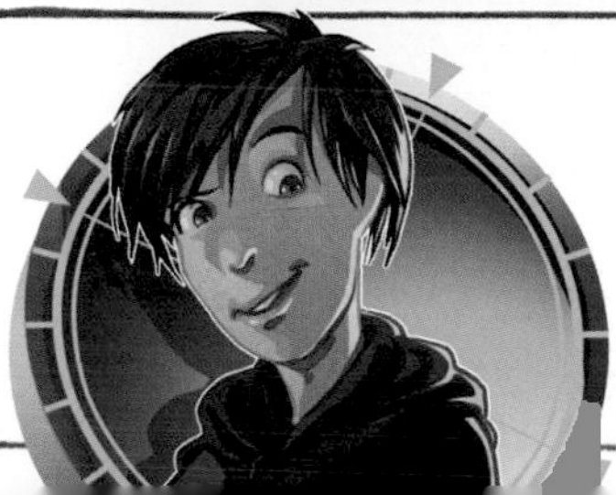

FLUX FACT

Spectral evidence played a big part in the trials. Witnesses presented dreams, visions, and other imagery as physical evidence. Witnesses could say the spirit of a witch appeared and hurt them. Their statements would be taken as fact.

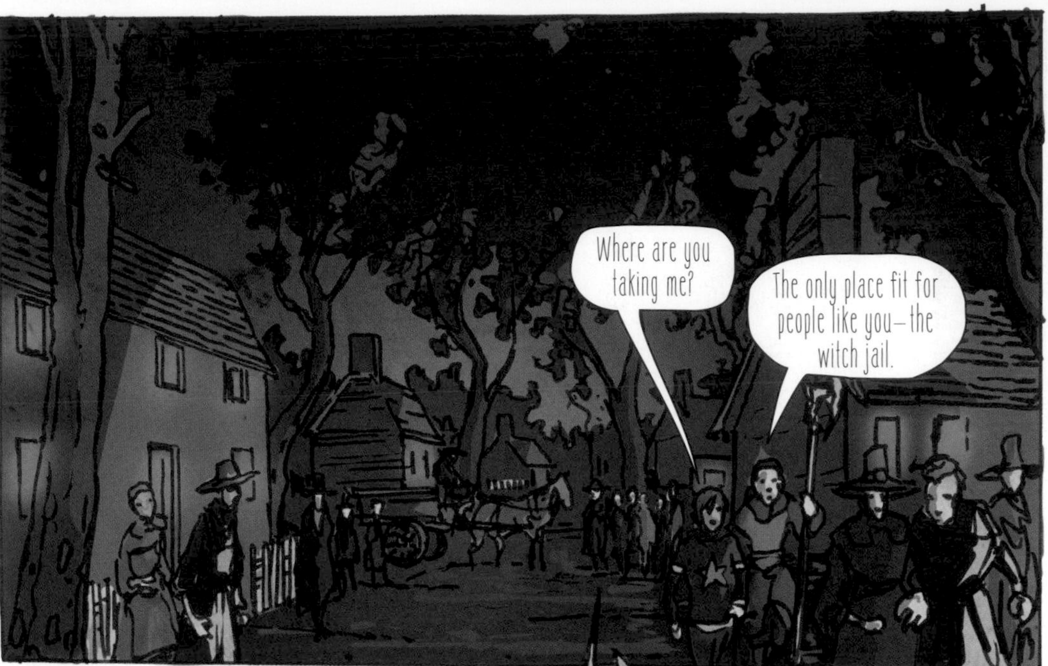
Where are you taking me?
The only place fit for people like you—the witch jail.

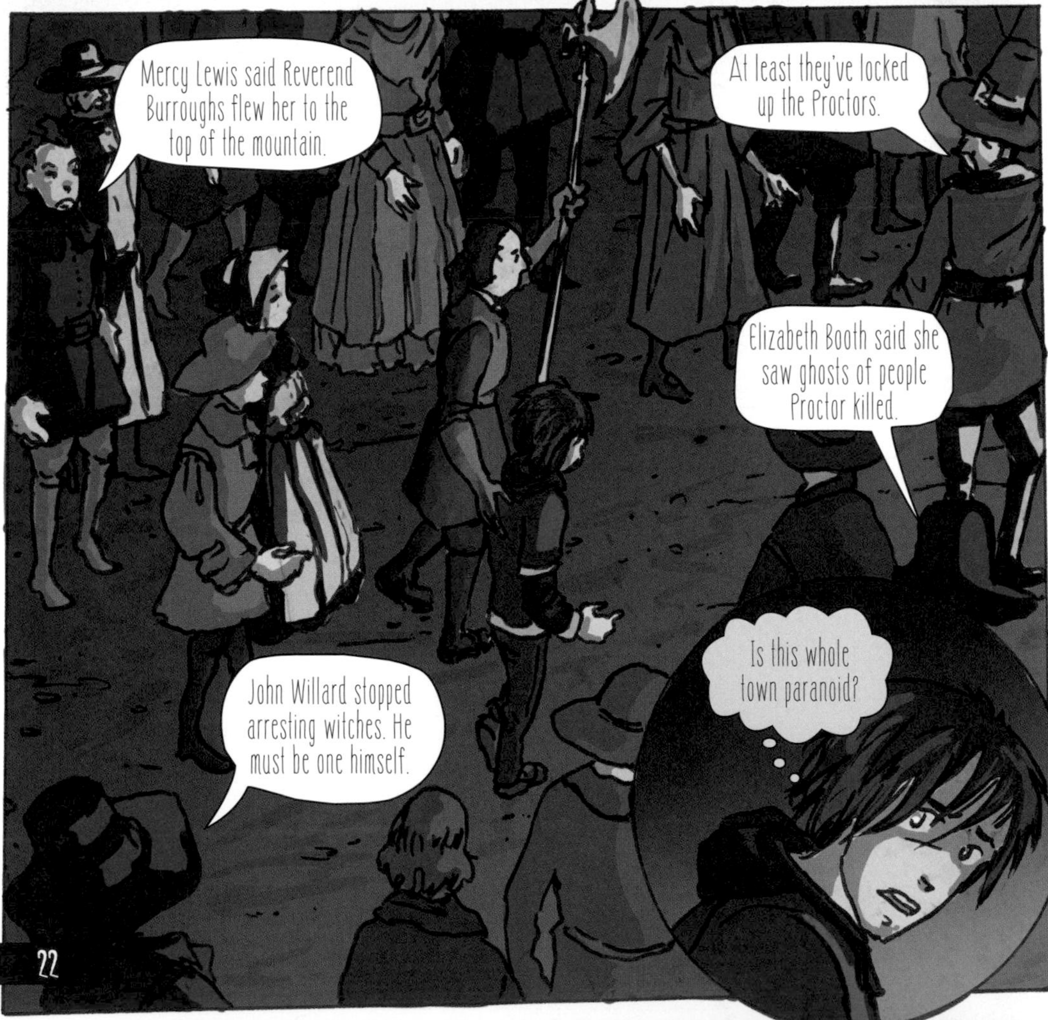
Mercy Lewis said Reverend Burroughs flew her to the top of the mountain.
At least they've locked up the Proctors.
Elizabeth Booth said she saw ghosts of people Proctor killed.
John Willard stopped arresting witches. He must be one himself.
Is this whole town paranoid?

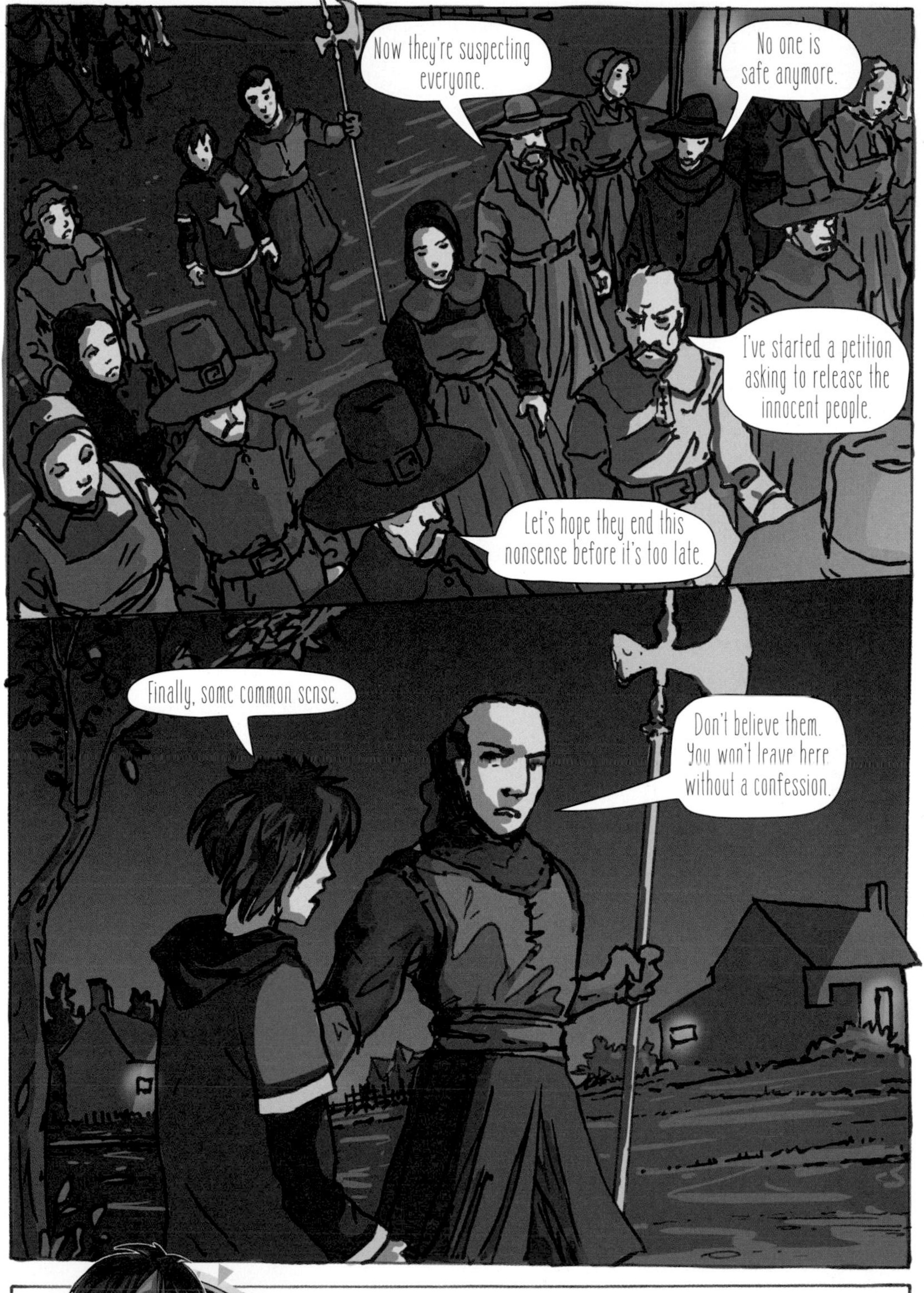
Now they're suspecting everyone.
No one is safe anymore.
I've started a petition asking to release the innocent people.
Let's hope they end this nonsense before it's too late.
Finally, some common scnsc.
Don't believe them. You won't leave here without a confession.

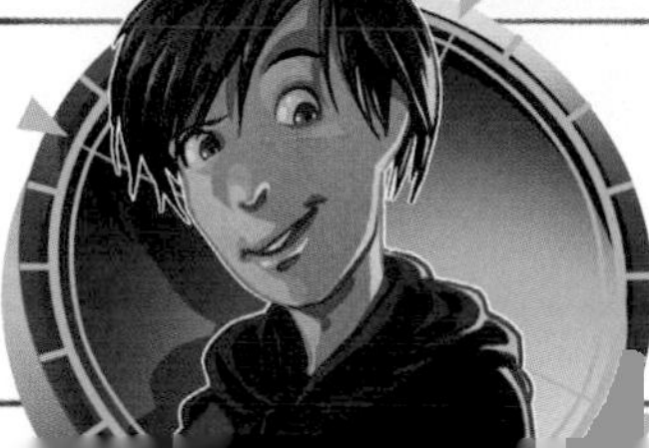

FLUX FACT

Judge Nathaniel Saltonstall was disgusted with the trials. He refused to take part in any after Bridget Bishop's. Later he was named as a witch.

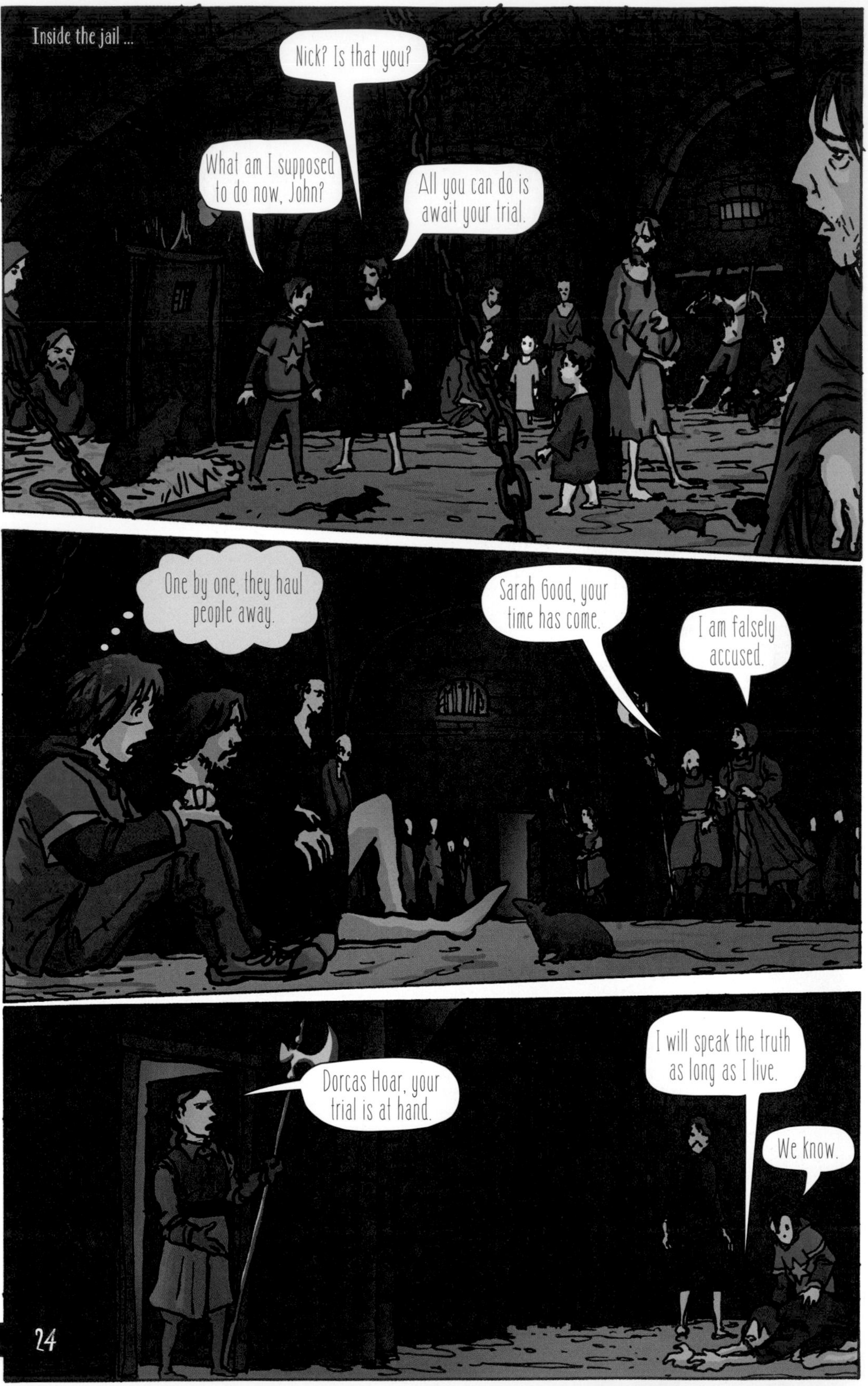
Inside the jail ...
Nick? Is that you?
What am I supposed to do now, John?
All you can do is await your trial.
One by one, they haul people away.
Sarah Good, your time has come.
I am falsely accused.
Dorcas Hoar, your trial is at hand.
I will speak the truth as long as I live.
We know.

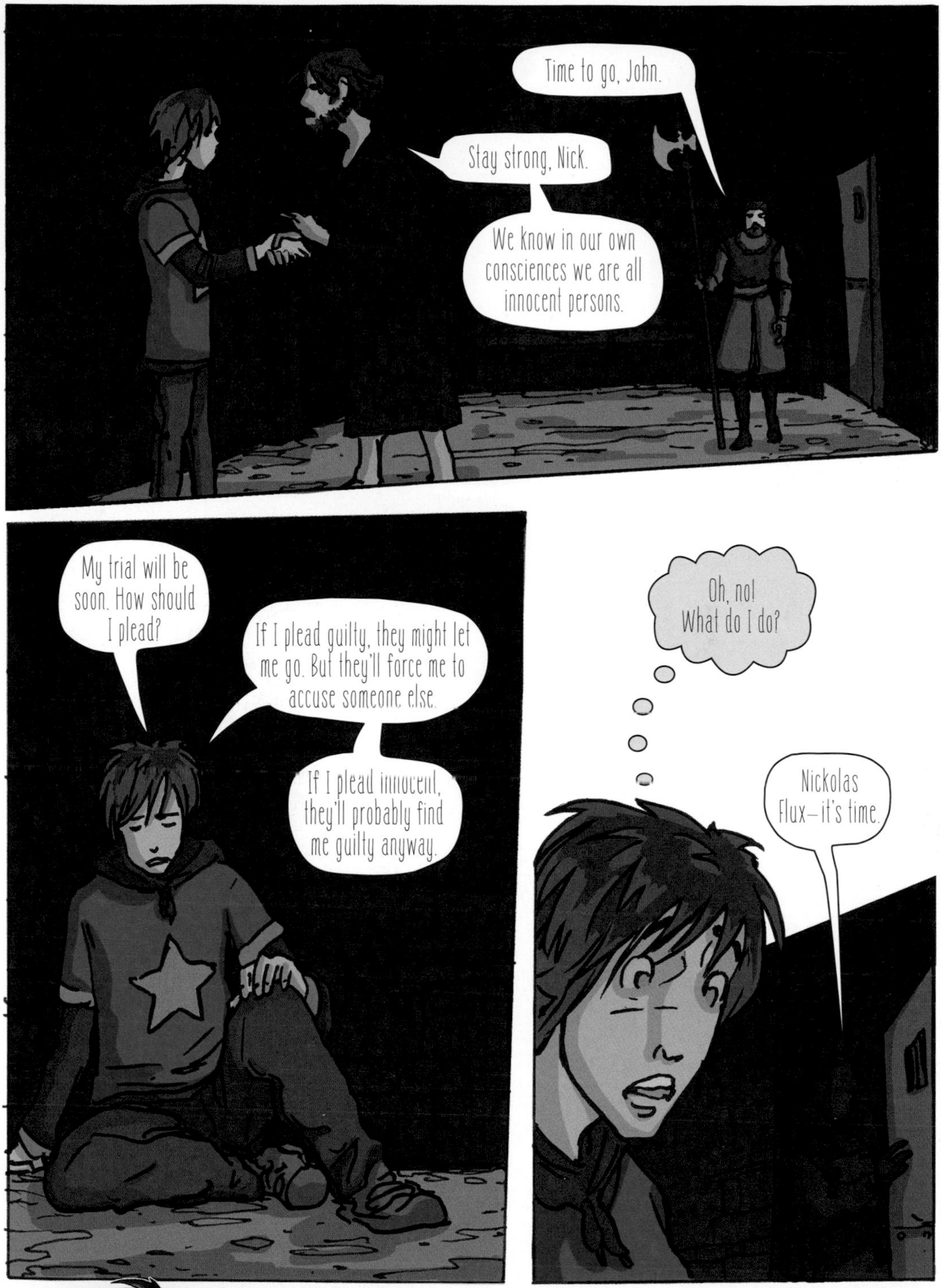
Time to go, John.
Stay strong, Nick.
We know in our own consciences we are all innocent persons.
My trial will be soon. How should I plead?
If I plead guilty, they might let me go. But they'll force me to accuse someone else.
If I plead innocent, they'll probably find me guilty anyway.
Oh, no! What do I do?
Nickolas Flux—it's time.

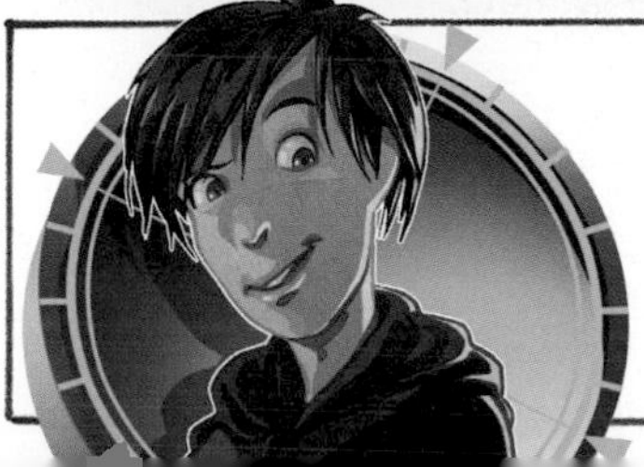

FLUX FACT

Nearly 50 people confessed to witchcraft. Their confessions were written and read at court. The confessions expressed remorse and named other witches.

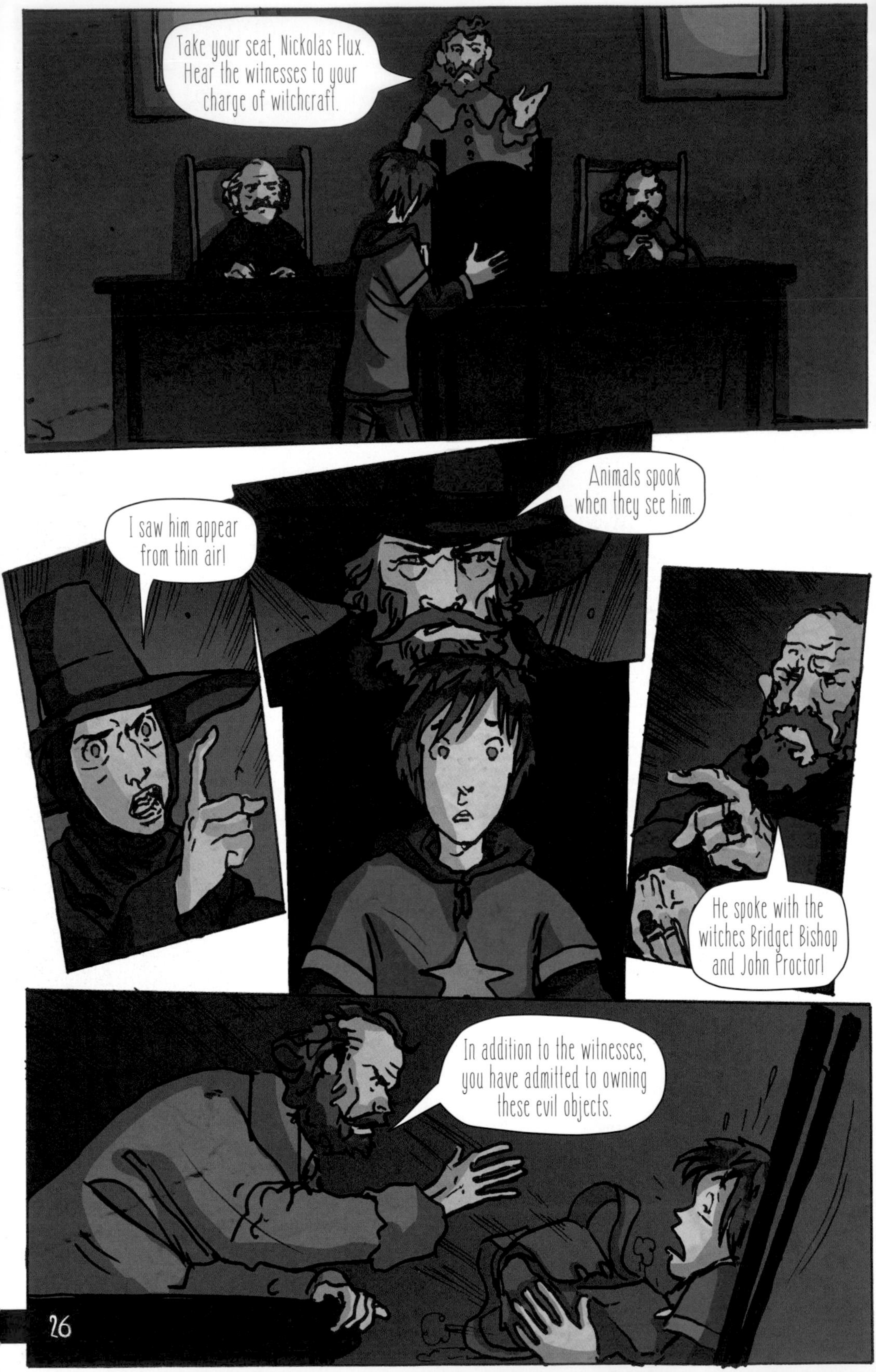
Take your seat, Nickolas Flux. Hear the witnesses to your charge of witchcraft.
Animals spook when they see him.
I saw him appear from thin air!
He spoke with the witches Bridget Bishop and John Proctor!
In addition to the witnesses, you have admitted to owning these evil objects.

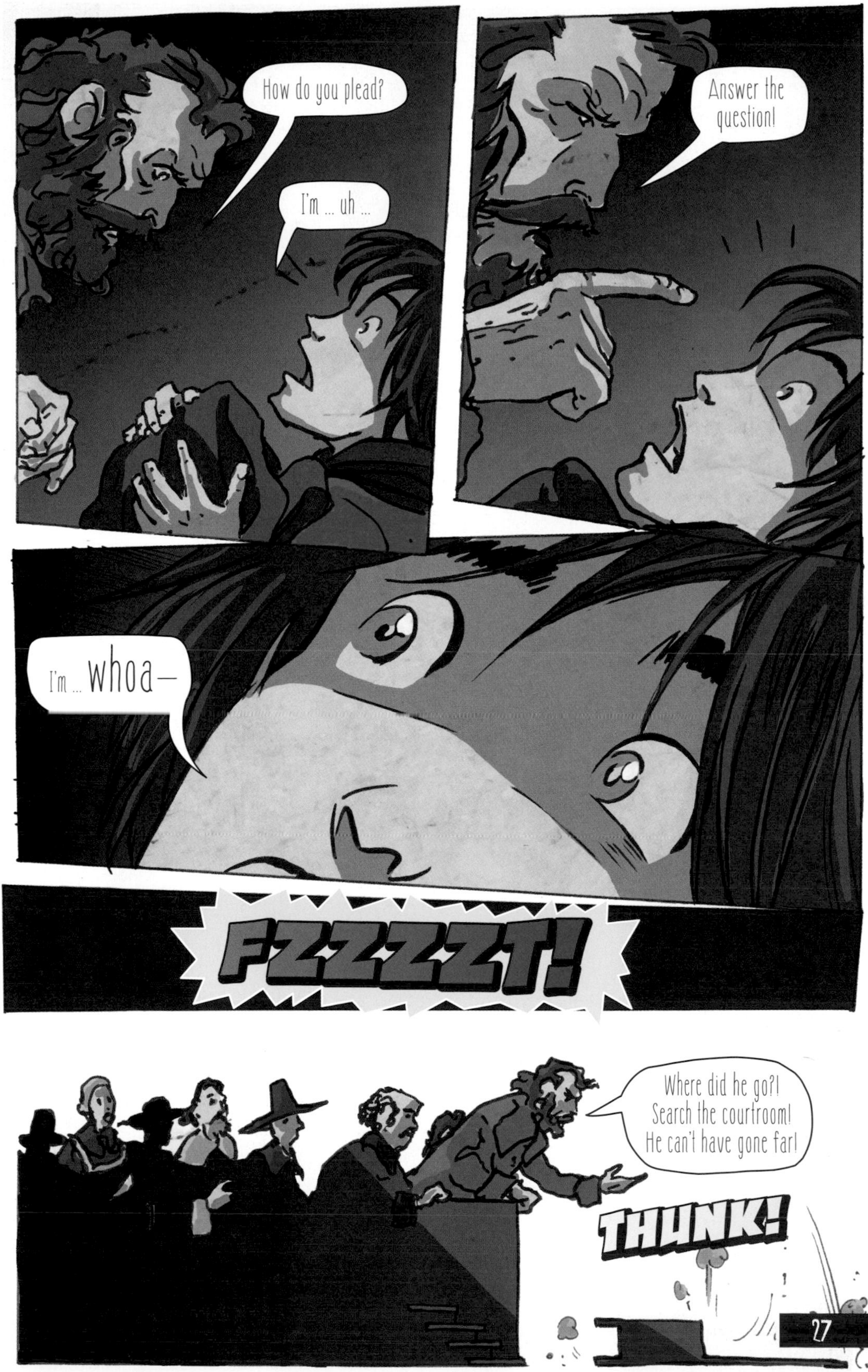
How do you plead?
I'm ... uh ...
Answer the question!
I'm ... whoa—
FZZZZZT!
Where did he go?! Search the courtroom! He can't have gone far!
THUNK!

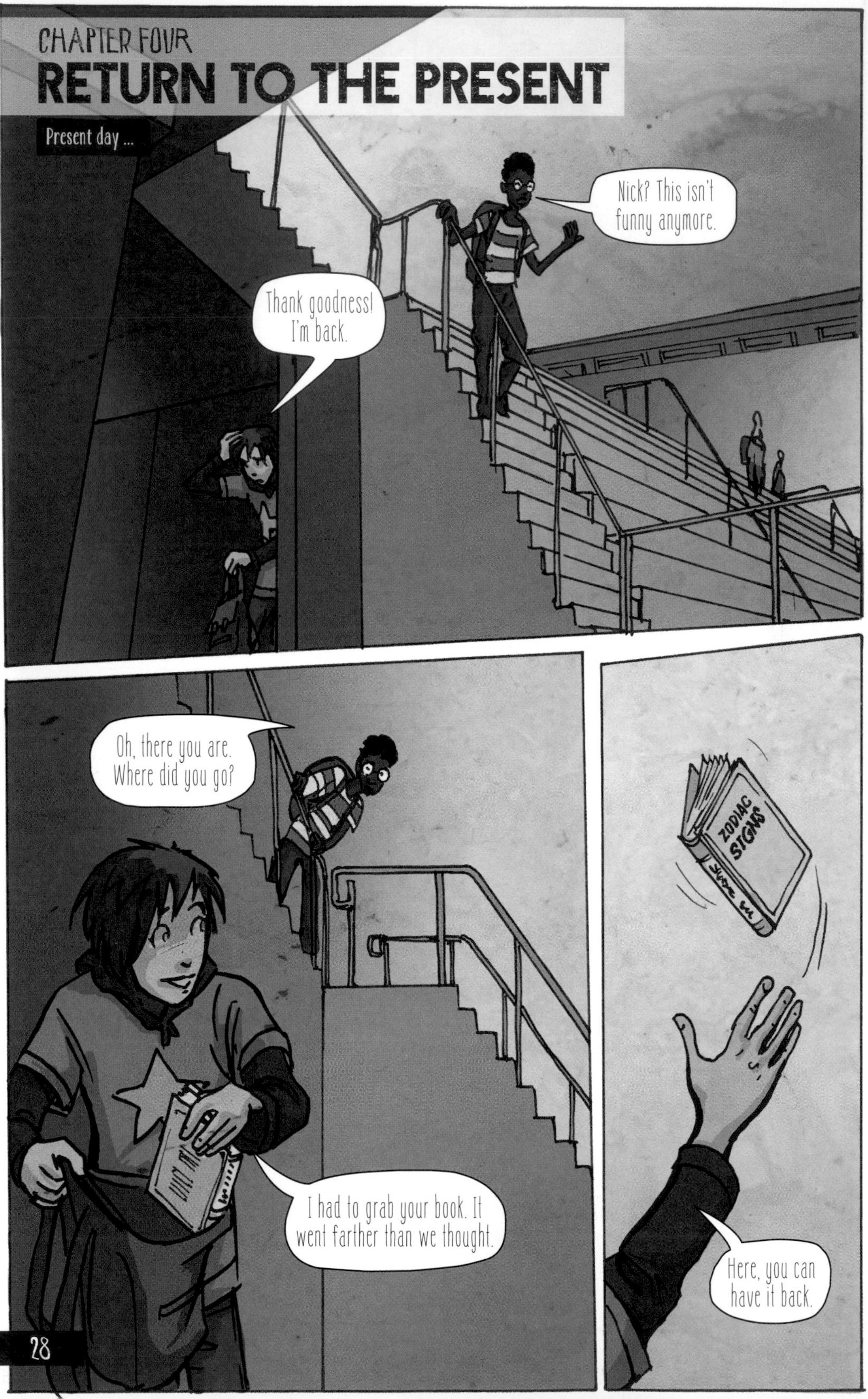
CHAPTER FOUR
RETURN TO THE PRESENT
Present day ...
Nick? This isn't funny anymore.
Thank goodness! I'm back.
Oh, there you are. Where did you go?
I had to grab your book. It went farther than we thought.
ZODIAC SIGNS
Here, you can have it back.

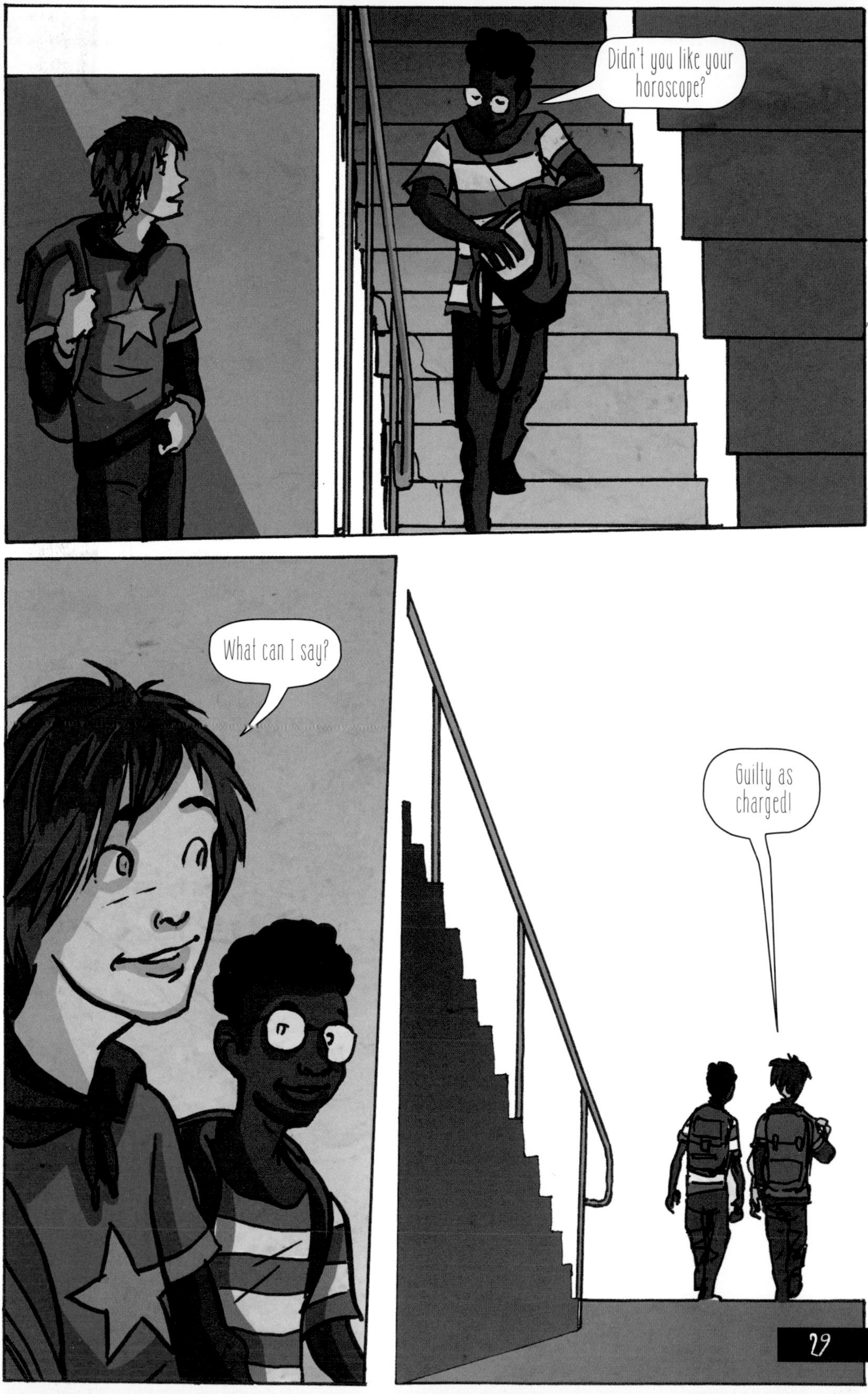
Didn't you like your horoscope?
What can I say?
Guilty as charged!

THE GIRLS OF SALEM

During the Salem Witch Trials, the affected girls were: Elizabeth (Betty) Parris, Abigail Williams, Ann Putnam, Mercy Lewis, Elizabeth Hubbard, Mary Walcott, and Mary Warren. They ranged in age from 9 to 19 years old.

THEORIES ON THE ACCUSATIONS

There are many theories about the seven girls and the attacks they suffered. They include epilepsy, emotional stress, child abuse, teenage boredom, and family feuds. One theory believes the girls were poisoned by ergot, a fungus that grows on rye. Ergot can cause seizures and hallucinations.

THE PUTNAMS

The Putnam family played a big role in the trials. Ann Putnam herself accused 19 people of witchcraft. Her father, Thomas Putnam, got warrants against many accused witches and gave evidence against them. He also recorded the afflictions of the accused girls. His niece was Mary Walcott. Mercy Lewis worked for the family.

TARGETING WOMEN

Accused witches were mostly women. Some were independent women who felt men and women were equal. They were not afraid to confront their neighbors about debts or disputes. Others were outcasts from society. Still others had desirable property that would be easy to take once they were out of the way.

COTTON MATHER

Cotton Mather was a minister in Boston. He believed in witchcraft and the Devil. He encouraged the judges at Salem, some of whom were his friends, to allow spectral evidence.

CALLING WITNESSES

During trials, defendants could call witnesses and question their accusers to prove their innocence. However, they and their witnesses could not testify under oath or appeal the court's decisions.

THE PROCTORS

After the Proctors were jailed, the sheriff seized all their belongings. The three Proctor children were left with nothing. They were later charged with witchcraft.

JOHN WILLARD

Constable John Willard refused to arrest people he believed to be innocent. He fled Salem but was caught about 40 miles (64 kilometers) away. He was found guilty of witchcraft and hanged.

DORCAS GOOD

At 4 years of age, Dorcas Good was the youngest accused witch. Dorcas was jailed on March 4, 1692. She was not released until May 1693.

GLOSSARY

ACCUSE (uh-KYOOZ)—to say someone has done something wrong

ASTROLOGY (uh-STRAH-luh-jee)—the study of how the positions of the stars and planets affect people's lives

CONVICT (kahn-VIKT)—to declare someone guilty of committing a crime

HALLUCINATION (huh-LOO-suh-nay-shuhn)—to see something that is not really there

HOROSCOPE (HOR-uh-skope)—a reading of the position of the stars and planets and how they might affect a person's life

PETITION (puh-TISH-uhn)—a letter signed by many people asking leaders for a change

POSSESS (poh-ZESS)—to have complete power over someone or something

SEIZURE (SEE-zhur)—a sudden attack of illness, or a spasm

SPECTER (SPEK-tur)—a ghost

SPECTRAL EVIDENCE (SPEK-truhl EV-uh-duhnss)—dreams, visions, and other imagery presented in court as physical evidence

READ MORE

BENOIT, PETER. *The Salem Witch Trials.* Cornerstones of Freedom. New York: Children's Press, 2013.

SMITH, ANDREA P. *The Salem Witch Trials.* Jr. Graphic Colonial America. New York: PowerKids Press, 2012.

WAXMAN, LAURA HAMILTON. *Who Were the Accused Witches of Salem?: And Other Questions about the Witchcraft Trials.* Six Questions of American History. Minneapolis: Lerner Publications, 2012.

INTERNET SITES

FactHound offers a safe, fun way to find Internet sites related to this book. All sites on FactHound have been researched by our staff.

Here's all you do:

Visit *www.facthound.com*

Type in this code: 9781476539478

Super-cool stuff! Check out projects, games and lots more at **www.capstonekids.com**

INDEX

ABOUT THE AUTHOR

Mari Bolte is an author of children's books and a lover of history. A degree in anthropology has given her an appreciation for other people in other times. She lives in southern Minnesota with her husband and daughter.